HERE TO COMPETE

HERE TO COMPETE

THE INSIDE STORY OF **NEWCASTLE UNITED** AND THE ERA OF **EDDIE HOWE**

Pete Graves

WELBECK

Published in 2023 by Welbeck
An imprint of Welbeck Non-Fiction Limited
Part of the Welbeck Publishing Group
Offices in: London – 20 Mortimer Street, London W1T 3JW &
Sydney – 205 Commonwealth Street, Surry Hills 2010, Australia
www.welbeckpublishing.com

A CIP catalogue record for this book is available from the British Library.

ISBNs
Hardback – 9781802797718
eBook – 9781802797732

Typeset by seagulls.net

Printed in the UK

10 9 8 7 6 5 4 3 2

Dedicated to

Steph for continued love and support,

our mini-magpies Will, Poppy and Daisy,

my Mum and Dad for first introducing me to St James' Park,

& dear Bex, Sim and Sare for putting up

with a footy-mad little brother.

Contents

INTRODUCTION

If you're reading this, then wow. Thank you so much for buying the book. Actually, double wow because it means I've actually finished writing it. Which in itself is an absolute bloody miracle. The truth is I've never felt like I've had a book in me. Books are written by academics and journalists who have a real way with words and phrases. I'm just a lad from Northumberland who got immensely lucky and ended up becoming a TV presenter. And I do love doing what I do, but without doubt the two main loves in my life are my family and Newcastle United. Just don't ask me to say which one means more.

Like every other kid my age, I was glued to the telly watching Bobby Robson's England team make it to the Italia 90 World Cup semi-final before getting knocked out by Germany on penalties. I cried for the best part of a week after seeing Chris Waddle's pen sail over the bar. In fact, all I talked about for weeks after that heartbreaking night in my living room was football and, looking back now, I must have done my family's head in. I kept asking my dad to take me to a football match. I was absolutely hooked on the idea of being inside an actual stadium. I suppose the dream would have been to go and watch England play, but Wembley was a long, long way from Newcastle. So, he suggested taking us to

St James' Park. Even though my dad was from Wigan, I grew up 20 minutes outside Newcastle and I remember my dad telling me that Bobby Robson, Paul Gascoigne, Peter Beardsley and Chris Waddle were all from the North East like me and that I might one day play in a World Cup, too. That was it for me – my life plan was sorted. Little Pete Graves would become the best footballer in the world and there was absolutely nothing that could possibly stand in my way. The only slight stumbling block for this eight-year-old dreamer was my actual football ability, which was average at best.

Before I go on, I want to reassure you that this book isn't about me. That would be the worst book in history and it probably wouldn't be very long either. This is a book about being in love with Newcastle United and, more importantly, the power of the club when it truly connects with the supporters. It's an idea that I had when the club was going through a really dark period, but I'm delighted that as I sit here writing this now, the club is back in a really great place.

I suppose I'm also trying to justify why I'm in a decent position to talk about Newcastle United with a bit of knowledge and authority. In my lifetime as a fan, there haven't been as many moments as I'd like where I could say that Newcastle United were a team we could be proud of. I mean we've basically won nothing except for a few second-tier league titles, for crying out loud. Don't anyone dare argue about the Intertoto Cup. But these years of hurt are disappearing into a distant memory. We've just qualified for the Champions League for the first time in 20 years. It feels surreal to say that. Our club is hopefully about to launch into orbit, and you know what, after the misery of the Mike Ashley era, our fans bloody deserve it more than anyone. It goes to show what can happen when the players, the manager, the backroom staff, the board, the owners – and the fans – are all United.

CHAPTER 1

THE **CATHEDRAL** **ON** THE **HILL**

Under our Christmas tree, in December 1990, I noticed a card for me. At first, in truth, I felt a bit short-changed. Where's the present?! And then I opened the card. It felt a bit heavier than a normal card. And that's because inside it were two tickets to see Newcastle United v Derby County at St James' Park in the third round of the FA Cup.

I was bouncing off the walls. My first Newcastle United game. I couldn't believe it and what made it even more special was that my dad was really excited, too. He'd never been to a football match either. This was something we were going to do together and it would become the start of a tradition that would change both of our lives. My dad was more of a cricket fan than a football fan as a young lad, heading off to see Lancashire county games with my grandad. But my enthusiasm for football had a big impact on my family and my dad in particular. I can understand that now, being a father myself, how your kids' passions for things have a profound impact on your life. So, after Italia 90, my dad got properly involved in football, and it was something we did together. And then somewhere along the way, my mum got caught up in it, too. Now my mum and dad go to every Newcastle United home game. They've got season tickets in the Milburn Stand (the 'main' stand), named after Jackie Milburn, the club legend who helped us win three FA Cups in the 1950s. My parents know all the people that sit around them – they've all been largely the same folks for years, so they all check in with each other, have a chat before and after the game, you know the sort of thing. They're not really bothered about sitting in the fancy seats and having a meal and all that corporate stuff. They like the atmosphere and the feeling of belonging and the community spirit. For them it has become a way of life.

I was so excited as my dad drove us to the stadium that cold Saturday afternoon. I say 'drove us to the stadium' – we actually parked about two miles away and I can remember seeing cars parked for miles and miles. That was back in the days where there'd be a whole load of local kids hanging around saying, 'Couple of quid to watch your car, mate?' My dad paid them all off as we walked towards the ground until we were far enough away from the car that the kids wouldn't know which car was ours. That memory reminds me of an urban myth that did the rounds about one of the local kids saying, 'Couple of quid to watch your car, mate?' and the guy responds with: 'Nah, it's all right, my dog's in there,' and the kid comes back with: 'Can your dog put out fires?!'

As we walked to the ground, I can still remember the yeasty smell that must have come from the famous Tyne Brewery nearby. As an eight-year-old, I thought it smelled terrible, but I grew to love it because it became forever associated with going to watch United play. And if I'm ever near a brewery, it always takes me to that long walk with my dad to St James'. On the way, Dad told me that England players Peter Shilton and Mark Wright would both be playing for the opposition. I couldn't believe that I was actually going to see a couple of my Italia 90 World Cup heroes in the flesh, and I think that's what excited me most, if I'm honest.

It's a tale as old as time, but my story is the same as the other young kids who are lucky enough to be taken to the football. You see St James' Park for the first time and you don't realise you're walking around with your mouth wide open. It's a unique stadium. It's literally the beating heart of Newcastle, and I can't think of another ground that is both so central to the city and seems like it's been there forever. It feels like you can see it everywhere you look in Newcastle. People want to talk about football everywhere you go, from old grannies to little kids. Football is part of the fabric of the city. The city has one club and the city has one sport. It's different to another one-football-club city like Leeds, because they've got Yorkshire County Cricket Club and the Leeds Rhinos rugby team, so football doesn't occupy quite the same religious-type fervour as it does in the Toon.

I held my dad's hand and we emerged from the stairs and I saw the pitch for the first time. I still remember that precise moment and how it made me feel to this very day. I mean, how weird is that? My mind has forgotten half the crap that's happened to me, but that precise moment remains ingrained. The grass seemed so green and perfect. It looked so much better than it did on the telly. I was instantly hooked. I imagine a few of you reading this will know exactly what I mean.

We were in the Milburn Stand (actually really close to where my parents have season tickets now – they might even be the same seats), and the ground at that time still had a cinder track around the outside of the actual pitch. I remember seeing the Newcastle United players warming up, even though I spent most of my time looking at Peter Shilton and Mark Wright. But the moment I remember the most was when we scored and the whole place erupted. Everyone was going absolutely mad, and after you get past the initial *What the hell is happening?* moment, you just embrace the mayhem. It just surpassed anything I could have possibly imagined. The singing, the atmosphere, that unique collective spirit, everything just got a hold of me and it's never left. And when things were dying down a bit in the stand, I looked up at the scoreboard and the 0 turned to a 1, and then an awful early 1990s pixelated image of Micky Quinn came up. Needless to say, I couldn't give a monkeys about Peter Shilton by that point. New heroes had emerged in my little mind and they all played for Newcastle United.

The player that stood out the most was Mick Quinn, our number 9 and the scorer of the first goal I saw at St James' Park. I'm so pleased it was Mick that scored it – a sensational lob on the half-volley past England's number one keeper. I still speak to Mick on occasion and he knows how much I love him for that moment. I remember him posting a tweet in 2015 with a video of the goal and saying, 'Here is Pete Graves' first-ever game. A third-round FA Cup victory for the Toon v Derby. I loved scoring past Shilts.' When I saw the post I just thought to myself, *If I could tell my eight-year-old self that my hero would one day be talking about me at that game, his head would have exploded.* But at that time, after seeing the net bulge, all I could think was how I'd be nabbing Quinn's number 9 shirt before too long.

After that match, my dad and I went to home games on Saturday afternoons. St James' Park had become instantly sacred to me; it was a religion, really – making the weekly pilgrimage to the 'cathedral on the hill', the famous nickname for St James' Park. I ended up with the other kids at the front of the Milburn Stand by the advertising hoardings. And if Newcastle United scored, the kids would just spill out on to the cinder track. Sometimes you'd just jump over on to the track and quickly run back like a kind of dare, excited that you were doing something a bit naughty. I still remember picking up the track's little orange pebbles. Some of the kids near me would wing them at the legs of the opposition play-ers when they were trying to take a corner. The throws were a bit half-hearted and none of them would actually make contact, but it felt like it was part of the routine that you did with the opposition. I definitely went on to the pitch a few times after full-time in later games and always in the last home game of the season, along with everyone else. No one tried to stop you then – it just felt like an end-of-season ritual.

Some people get a few slices of luck in life and that was certainly the case for me as I grew up. But my lucky streak seemed to ramp up the more time I spent following Newcastle United. I was born in Hexham, about 20 miles west of Newcastle, which is where lots of the players lived at the time, so I used to see my hero Mick Quinn and many of the others at the local supermarket.

Their hearts must have sunk when they saw me approaching them. I always had my autograph book in my back pocket and it didn't matter how may signatures I had – I always asked them to sign it again.

I remember going up to Mick Quinn one summer outside Safeway and saying to him how well he'd done on some pre-season tour in Norway. He told me he'd scored 11 goals on the tour and I said, 'I know – I hope you carry that form into the upcoming season.' He must have thought I was an odd child. I mean I was about 10 years old and I was fully aware of our pre-season form in a world that was pre-internet. I'm not even sure how I knew about the pre-season tour, but I remember my dad would buy the local newspapers every day and I'd cut out the articles about the club and stick them in my scrapbook, so it must have been a column in one of those. I couldn't get enough of *Roy of the Rovers* either as a young lad. (For you younger readers, it was a weekly comic strip about fictional player Roy Race, of equally fictional Melchester Rovers.) I even started drawing my own cartoon strip on the back of the *Roy of the Rovers* comic, and I called it 'Quinn' after my hero. When I was a bit older, I'd go out and buy the two big football weekly magazines: *Match* and *Shoot!* as soon as they came out.

The really sad thing was that the scrapbooks that I'd spent bloody ages putting together ended up getting destroyed in a flood at my parents' house. Not just a little flood, either; we're talking water-above-head-height kind of thing. And my football scrapbooks and autograph books were in a cupboard in the front room along with all our family photo albums and our music collection. My football kits and sports stuff was in the cupboard under the stairs. Everything was completely trashed. My mum was in bits. When the water finally subsided, the whole house was covered in silt and you could see where the water came up to in the room. Luckily, I kept my two most precious autograph books in my room, so they survived.

Like every other kid in Newcastle, you fancied yourself as a number 9 and everything was about who scored the goals. I didn't care about anything else. These days, I see my 11-year-old William, and he's as happy with a really good pass or a strong tackle as he is about scoring a goal. Maybe that reflects how the number 9 position has changed now, and you don't get that many out-and-out old-school number 9s. It's more about the attacking midfielders, who can dance around players, make that perfectly weighted pass and score 25-yard screamers. Micky Quinn wasn't that sort of player. You'd find him in the box and he always seemed to be in the right place at the right time to stick it in the back of the net. Sometimes it would bounce in off his shin. He didn't care and nor did I!

Mick Quinn banged in 34 goals in his first season in black and white. It was the start of my adoration for anyone who's played up front for Newcastle United. And to be fair, we had some amazing strikers. The guys who have worn that number 9 shirt include three of the top 11 all-time Premier League top scorers: Les Ferdinand, Andy Cole and Alan Shearer.

People sometimes ask me if I get nervous about meeting and interviewing famous people. Well, I've been lucky enough to meet loads of sporting icons, but chatting to Callum Wilson recently – I dropped my phone on the floor twice in front of him while I was giving him my number! It reminded me how weird I get when I'm in the company of Newcastle United players, more than I would be if I was about to chat to someone like Lionel Messi or Cristiano Ronaldo. I think I just revert to being that eight-year-old boy again, seeing my heroes in black and white for the first time and feeling helplessly in love. Mad I know.

Later that 1990–91 season, another slice of football-related luck would fall my way. For some unknown reason the club photographer randomly picked me out of the crowd and took a photo of me, which appeared front and centre on the match-day programme the following week. It caused quite a stir in my local village and, of course, I lapped up the attention. I convinced myself the photographer must have sensed that I was a future Newcastle United legend and he was getting some early shots in that he could sell for millions of pounds later down the line when I broke Jackie Milburn's goalscoring record. I remember thinking that the next game I went to everyone would obviously know who I was and maybe I'd be asked to sign a few autographs just like the players. Much to my disappointment, not one person said a word. But the whole experience just deepened my obsession with Newcastle United.

CHAPTER 2

ARISE, **KING KEV**

ooking back now, I think 1991 was the perfect time to start
watching Newcastle United. I had a season's run-in to get me
properly hooked before Kevin Keegan took over and the whole
place went mental. What I didn't appreciate at the time was that
the past couple of years before 1991 had been pretty shocking.
Not only had we been relegated in the 1988–89 season, we
finished bottom of the table by some distance, only winning seven
games in the league all season and crashing out of both cups early.
We'd also lost two of our best players – Paul Gascoigne to Spurs
and Peter Beardsley to Liverpool – the season before. Whenever a
team goes down, you want to be bouncing straight back. But that
didn't happen in 1989–90. We got close, but Leeds and Sheffield
United secured the automatic promotion places with one game
to play, so we finished in third – left to the lottery of the play-
offs. Limping into the play-offs in sixth place were our arch-rivals,
Sunderland, and so we'd face them in the play-off semi-final. You
couldn't make it up. At the time it was dubbed the 'biggest Tyne–
Wear derby in history'.

After a goalless draw in the first leg at Roker Park, which
wasn't without incident – our keeper John Burridge saving a
last-minute penalty from left-back Paul Hardyman, who was so

annoyed about it that he booted Burridge in the head afterwards, earning him a red – they came to St James' Park three days later. And we started well, hitting the post nine minutes in, but against the run of play Sunderland scored from a low cross four minutes later. Under sustained pressure, which drew some good saves from their keeper Tony Norman, we couldn't find a way through, and to add insult to injury, Marco Gabbiadini scored in the 86th minute to make it 2–0 to Sunderland. A pitch invasion followed, from our fans, which might have actually been a sneaky way to try and force the ref to abandon the game. The referee sent both lots of players to their dressing rooms while the police tried to restore order. Twenty minutes later, the last few minutes were played out and we'd been condemned to another season in the Second Division, and at the hands of Sunderland. Gutting.

Manager Jim Smith didn't last that much longer. In his first season in charge we'd been relegated, but the club stuck with him in a way that just wouldn't have happened today. And although he brought us close to going up, things behind the scenes weren't great. The boardroom was all over the place and Smith had almost nothing to work with transfer cash-wise. He resigned in March 1991, famously branding the club 'unmanageable' largely in reference to an ongoing boardroom tussle. The board took a gamble on Argentinian World-Cup-winning player turned young manager, Ossie Ardiles. He was a name that I was familiar with, and the fans got quite excited about what he'd bring to St James' Park. Ossie had made a name for himself in his first managerial appointment, at Swindon Town, by ditching the long-ball game in favour of a 4–4–2 diamond shape, playing attacking football and keeping the ball on the deck. He was the first foreign manager in Newcastle United's history but the gamble didn't pay off.

It wasn't a great time under Ossie, mainly because we were getting beaten pretty much every week and spent most of the time in the bottom half of the Second Division, at one point looking like relegation to the third tier might be on the cards. My French teacher at school, Mr Sugden, absolutely loved Ossie, though, and we used to chat about football a lot. He kept insisting that Ossie just needed a bit more time, and it'd all come good. But he was running out of games to turn things around. To Ossie's credit, he did blood a lot of promising young local lads and gave game time to some of the local rising stars. Local boy Lee Clark came up through the youth system and was only 18 when he made his debut in 1989. Steve Howey had been brought in in December 1989 and was only 19. Steve Watson made his debut in November 1990 coming off the bench aged 16 and 223 days, the youngest player ever to appear for Newcastle United. Steve Howey told a great little story about the time Ossie had the first eleven playing on a full-sized pitch against no one – a training session known as shadow play. Here's how it went:

'So, Ossie has set us up, we've taken the kick-off, passed it back to Lee Clark, Lee Clark's passed it back to Kevin Scott, again we're playing backwards and we should be playing forwards cos we aren't playing against anybody. Kevin Scott gives it to Steve Watson, Steve Watson turns round and passes it back to Tommy Wright who's in goal, but Tommy Wright was putting his gloves on in the back of the net, and the ball goes in the goal. We're getting beat 1–0 and we ain't playing any f****r.'

Ossie was sacked in February 1992 after a 5–2 defeat against relegation rivals Oxford United, with the team in 20th place, looking like relegation to the Third Division was happening. Ossie even invited the press into his house on the day of his sacking, with his wife Silvia making cups of tea for the assembled photographers and journalists. Sir John Hall, the chairman of the board, called it 'the hardest decision I've ever had to make in my life, in my business life, and I have very mixed emotions, but I have to get on with the job and move forward now.' And move forward he did, because the next decision he made was one of the best in the history of the club. And you'd think that after Ossie, Hall would have gone for a safe pair of hands to steer the club through choppy waters. A Roy Hodgson-type caretaker figure. But that wasn't what he had in mind. He wanted a club legend who'd last been seen on the pitch at St James' Park leaving the ground in a helicopter dressed in his kit.

In my lifetime, there have been four managers that the fans have genuinely loved. Kevin Keegan was the first. I'd always known his name in my house before his appointment because my mum and Kevin were both from Doncaster and went to the same school. I remember my mum had nipped into Newcastle to do some shopping while I was in the car on my own. I flicked the radio on just as they announced that Kevin Keegan had agreed to take over as manager. It was the local radio station and the presenters were really excited. It felt straight away like this was massive news. And that day my dad came back from work, opened the door, and the first thing he said was: 'Bloody hell – Keegan's the new manager!' My dad is from Wigan and has a soft spot for Liverpool FC, where Keegan made his name in the 1970s, so he was thrilled. He told me why this was such a big deal for Newcastle United, a former club legend and England captain coming to manage them. He told me all about the way he left the stadium in his kit after his final game at St James' Park, and I thought to myself, *This guy doesn't seem human. It's like Superman's turned up in black and white instead of red and blue.*

No one questioned that he'd never managed a club before. It didn't matter. We watched him on the news that day, and the way he spoke, you just instantly loved the guy, talking about how Newcastle United was potentially the biggest club in Great Britain. And then they played the clip of his first game as a Newcastle United player in 1982, where he heads it down for himself from a flick-on and puts away a one-on-one with the keeper, sliding it into the bottom right corner. And then he jumps straight into the Gallowgate End and stays there for ages celebrating with the fans. Alan Shearer was one of the kids in the Gallowgate for that game and here are his memories of Keegan's debut and how it feeds into his feelings going to St James' Park in 2023:

'I remember queuing up at the Gallowgate as an 11-year-old in 1982 for Keegan's debut for four or five hours beforehand and I remember the atmosphere as if it were yesterday. I know it was totally different then because it was all standing up, but I remember being crushed and losing all my mates. The atmosphere then was what it's like now [in 2023]. I'm back to being that 11-year-old kid again when the atmosphere's amazing. I had it then as a boy, I had it later as a player under Kevin and Sir Bobby and now back to being a fan and watching it, I'm enjoying it and loving it again.'

I've been lucky enough to get to know Kevin really well and he's just got a way about him that makes everyone that he speaks to feel amazing. When he became the manager of the football club in 1992, hope had returned to St James' Park.

Here's what Kevin told me about taking the job: 'I think it would have been a gamble [taking the job] had I not played for the club, but having played for the club for two years and witnessed the promotion year [1983–84] and what it was like, I had a bit of an insight into the club. It wasn't like I was going into the unknown, like when I went to Hamburg, for example. I was going back to somewhere that I knew – I knew what the fans wanted when we played – this desire to see us get forward and not really pass it back too much. So I wasn't going in cold. I was down in Hampshire living in Romsey – I had a farm – and John Hall was on the phone and the first words he said were: "Kevin, the two people that can save Newcastle United are on the phone." He said, "I've got the money and you've got the passion." And I said, "I'll do it." I never thought about the implications, I mean, I lived in Hampshire, my kids were in school down there, but I said yes. I took it on and I think the club were third bottom when I took over, and had never been relegated to the Third Division. I knew a few of the Newcastle players, but I didn't know all of them and I certainly didn't know any of the opposition, so it was a gamble, but to me it was like, *Well I'll have a go, let's just see if we can stay up.*'

It was a far bigger task than I think even Kevin imagined though when he took it on. On his first day in the job, he came up with a plan with what had to change.

'Don Revie [the former player and Leeds and England manager] used to say "chip, chip". If you want to break a rock up, you don't just get a sledgehammer, you chip away at it and then it crumbles when you get so far. So I started chip-chipping. I went to the training ground and it was a disgrace, there's no other word for it. I left it [as a player] in 1984, and went back in 1992 and I couldn't believe it. Nobody had done anything to the place except sell some of the land for houses, so the training ground that I trained on, which was very poor back then, was even worse. The changing rooms weren't clean, the gym was a disgrace. I couldn't believe it. The first thing I did was go to the chairman and I said to him, "I want to spend a few grand on doing up the dressing rooms, showers and cleaning it." He said, "What will that do?" and I said, "Well, it'll make players, when they come in, feel like there's a bit of pride in the club, you know?"

'So first of all, we painted it. I think we played Bristol City on the Saturday [after I started], won the game and the painters and the cleaners had already moved in to get it back respectable, clean the tiles, clean the gym out – there were old sandwich packets all over the back of the gym equipment, odd socks, I couldn't believe it. We'd got a good start with the win against Bristol City and when the players came in on the Tuesday, they said,

"Cor – look at this!" When I got them together before training I said to the lads, "You'll notice a few changes already. That's the start. The next thing is, if you get results, we're not going to be travelling to games on the day of the match any more," which is what they were doing. I think the players had this mentality that no one really cared about them. The club had just lost its way. And you can't blame Ossie [Ardiles] or the chairman, it was a combination of things.'

His first game as Newcastle United manager was against Bristol City on 8 February 1992. The atmosphere was absolutely unbelievable at St James' Park – the whole place was buzzing. Usually, at home games, I'd be standing with the other kids at the Milburn paddock and there was loads of space around. We'd even be kicking footballs around during the game. But at this game, the whole place was rammed. The kids in the stands, including me, were crowd-surfing (we didn't have any choice about it!) and being plonked out at the front of the stand. I ended up sitting on a wall and had no idea where my dad was. It was the first time I'd actually felt a bit uncomfortable at the sheer number of people occupying the space. And then Kevin Keegan walked through the tunnel in his black-and-white tracksuit and the place erupted. All you could hear was noise and the flashing of camera bulbs from the press queued up on the touchline.

I remember being completely convinced we were going to win. Everyone in the ground was. And we didn't have any reason to be – we'd been getting battered most weeks and had gone four games without a win. But somehow that energy coursing around the place didn't fizzle out despite not scoring in the first half, and we came out in the second half and scored two in two minutes, with another five minutes after that. Keegan reacted just like any other fan for each goal, jumping about, screaming with joy, pumping his fists and hugging everyone around him. So did assistant manager Terry McDermott, Kevin's right-hand-man as assistant manager and also his former teammate at Liverpool and Newcastle. It was a fairy-tale homecoming and a fairy-tale win. St James' Park was alive again. He was one of us.

There were more twists and turns to come after that, though. We beat Sunderland at home the following month, which pleased the fans no end, but then we lost five in a row. Relegation loomed again. Then came what turned out to be the game I remember more than any other that season, a home game against Portsmouth. We had to win or we were down. Chance after chance kept going begging. Seventy-five minutes went by, then 80, then 85, and it just didn't seem like our day. And then David Kelly stepped up with another vital goal, this one a fantastic half-volley just five minutes from full-time. I was positioned right behind him from where I was standing, and it's one of those unique moments as a fan that you know it's in a fraction of a second before anyone else does. I watched it sail into that corner – an iconic goal in the history of the club – and it was the best goal I'd ever seen with my own eyes. The place went mad again and this time I was thrown on to the pitch and I'm running like crazy along with loads of other Newcastle United fans. You can tell how important that goal was because a ridiculously long banner appeared this season [2022–23] at the Gallowgate quoting the commentator on the game: 'Kelly – that'll do. You cannot put a price on that goal from David Kelly.'

It came down to the final day of the season. Losing that game against fourth-placed Leicester City at Filbert Street would consign us to the Third Division – the first time that would have ever happened. It was unthinkable. Gavin Peacock scored just before half-time, and for a while it seemed like we'd avoided relegation. But there was one final twist, as Steve Walsh scored for Leicester in the 89th minute. Nightmare. Cue a bunch of guys feverishly checking their pocket radios for live updates on the other teams in the relegation dogfight. But then, just a minute later, Walsh scored at the wrong end, sending Newcastle United fans into delirium. There's nothing like a great escape at the end of the season, although it does put a few more grey hairs on you. Our team wasn't that great that season, if I'm honest, but Keegan had harnessed the crowd, and that made a big difference to the outcome on the pitch. The whole city was behind him. It would be the same with the Bobby Robson era and Eddie Howe now: when the club has the supporters on board, it can do amazing things.

The following season started and the fans carried with us that energy from the last game. But no one could have predicted what that season would bring. It was a joke. We won the first 11 games of the season and it felt like we had the championship wrapped up by Christmas. Seven games into the season, we were playing Bristol City at home and my dad and I drove to the game, paid the lads hanging by the cars, and walked up to the stadium and round to the Milburn entrance, as per. But we got there and found a massive queue snaking back from the turnstiles. And when we were about five away from the front, they put a sign up saying 'Full'. I couldn't believe it! I'd built up the excitement for two weeks since the last home game. So we ran round to the Gallowgate and Leazes stands trying to find a turnstile that was letting people in but they were all closed. I couldn't understand what was happening. My dad tried to explain calmly that they couldn't fit any more people into the ground, but that wasn't going to work on me, so we tried to get in with the away fans. But we got a firm 'You're not from Bristol' from the security guys. It was hard to argue with the man when I was wearing a Newcastle United shirt. So we walked back to the car, completely despondent. There's nothing more frustrating than hearing the excitement in the ground when you can't see what's happening! We drove home in silence, both gutted, and listened to the game on the radio, which of course turned out to be the biggest win of the season so far, a 5–0 mauling. I was delighted that we'd won again, but there was a sadness in me that we'd not been there to see it. I turned to my dad and we both knew there was only one option. It was time to apply for a season ticket.

I recently showed my son William a YouTube clip of the eighth game of that season (and our eighth successive win), against Peterborough United – the singing, the chanting, everything was in perfect unison. The sheer noise – it was like someone had been hired to train the fans how to become one. It was extraordinary. My son watched it with an open mouth and said, 'Wow Dad, it's like an army', and he was right to say that. It was an army. The Toon Army. And there's nothing more powerful when it's in full voice.

In March 1993, Keegan broke the club record to sign Andy Cole for £1.75 million from Bristol City. Kevin was kind enough to tell me about the day he decided to sign him:

'We [Kevin and Terry McDermott] were in the office – it was about 4.30 in the afternoon on a Tuesday and we [were looking through] these lists of the fixtures. Back then we used to watch a lot of games. Unlike now when the managers of clubs don't go to many games – they've got people who assess and give them reports – but this was back in the day when your manager and team would do everything. One of the problems with Newcastle is you're a long way from everywhere, so if you're looking at going to a game and it's already 4.30, you're in trouble.

'Because we'd played Bristol City [the season before, at Ashton Gate] and Coley gave us a torrid time [memorably turning our captain, Kevin Scott, and leaving him flat on his arse], we said let's have a look at him again. So Terry Mac says, "You're not going to believe this – Bristol City are playing tonight." I said, "He's in Bristol, Terry, and we're in Newcastle. We ain't going to make it." Terry came back in about ten minutes later – we were looking for a game a bit nearer to go and watch. At that moment, Douglas Hall [son of the chairman, Sir John] popped his head around the door on the way to the boardroom and said, "Hi, boys, anything we can do for you?" And Terry said, "Yeah, we could do with borrowing that plane you use!" "What for?" Douglas asked. "We want to go to Bristol to watch this game tonight," Terry said. So Douglas got on his phone and his pilot was in Yarm [10 miles south-east of Middlesbrough], shopping. I only know that because he was absolutely livid about having to come and get the plane. We went down to Teesside Airport, and the pilot shot up from Yarm and got the plane out. We landed at Bristol where they'd fixed up a taxi for us, so we got to the ground and as we sat in the directors' box where they had seats for us, the teams were coming out. That's how it was. Incredible. He only played 20 minutes. He was injured – he had a big bandage on and came off – he couldn't run. Coming back, we get on the plane and Terry Mac says, "What a f***ing waste of time that was, gaffer!" And I said, "How many players would want to play when they're injured, Terry? So we know he's good and we know he's genuine. And we know he wanted to play even though he physically wasn't right. I like that – it's character." So we convinced ourselves he was the kind of player we wanted.'

Keegan respected Cole's desire to play, even though he was already carrying an injury. He thought he had courage, heart and determination, and that it said a lot about him as a player. So, off the back of that trip, he signed him.

The final game of the season was Leicester again, this time at home, and we battered them 7–1. It was 6–0 before half-time. It was the perfect indication of how far we'd come since last season. Two hat-tricks in the game. One from David Kelly and another from our new 21-year-old £1.75 million record signing from Bristol City in March 1993: Andy Cole. Rob Lee got the other one. Grown men were crying on the terraces. There was talk of the promised land of the Premier League. That game was shown live on telly, on ITV, which was kind of unheard of for us back then, but it led to a famous chant that's still sung today at St James' Park:

Andy Cole, Andy Cole, Andy Andy Cole,
he gets the ball and scores a goal, Andy Andy Cole

David Kelly, David Kelly, David David Kelly,
he scored a hat-trick on the telly, David David Kelly

Robbie Lee, Robbie Lee, Robbie Robbie Lee,
he scored a goal on ITV, Robbie Robbie Lee

Kelly had stepped up in another big game, and by then, he'd become my hero, the man that filled Micky Quinn's shoes as our number 9 after he left in November 1992. That was a big shock to the fans – Big Mick was our top scorer in the 1990–91 season, with 20 goals in all competitions, and our player of the season for 1990. He was a legend. But the same fate was dealt out to David Kelly in June 1993, this time sold to Wolves. Kelly had scored the only goal – a stunner – at St James' Park against Portsmouth when we were facing relegation in the penultimate game of the previous season [1991–92] and he scored the goal that secured promotion, against Grimsby on 4 May 1993. Kelly was our top scorer, with 28 goals across all competitions. Again, he was a legend. Our number 9s were coming thick and fast. But Kevin had a plan. He wanted young players with pace.

I always wanted to know why Micky Quinn (and David Kelly) left, so I asked Kevin in June 2023 and here's what he told me:

'We just had to make changes and I think sometimes it's easier to change the little things that don't make a big impact, but I felt we needed some more pace up front. Micky Quinn was the best finisher that I'd ever worked with. If [someone] put him in, he'd score, but you'd have to get him in. I saw a different way of playing. Football wasn't just relying on knocking it up to the centre-forward and he could just do a shuffle and score, so we started to look at players who had a bit of pace who could threaten teams. You look at most of the players we signed – Andy Cole, Les Ferdinand, John Beresford, Ruel Fox – and they all had pace. We were looking at playing in a quick way and Micky was unlucky. I see him a lot on the circuit now, and we have a laugh about it. The joke he tells about it is, "I went to see the gaffer, he told me I was playing and I scored. The next week I wasn't in the team so I knocked on the gaffer's door. 'Gaffer, I don't know whether I'm coming or going!' And I said, "You're going, Micky – I've just sold you to Coventry [for £250,000]." Sir John Hall questioned it, telling me that Micky had scored a lot of goals and that, but I told him, "Don't worry, Mr Chairman, we've got to find other ways of playing and I think he'll struggle to score goals in the Premier League." Well, Micky only scored a hat-trick on his debut against Arsenal! I remember the chairman coming in and saying, "He's scored three goals today, Kevin!"

As for David Kelly going, here's what Kevin told me: 'He could feel aggrieved as well [when I sold him] – he didn't do anything wrong, but we just wanted to make changes. Gavin Peacock as well. These were all, probably, in the fans' view, some of the outstanding players of that era, but we weren't third bottom of the division for no reason [in 1991–92]. We weren't good enough but also, they were the players that we could get money for.'

Meanwhile, new boy Andy Cole was getting better and better, scoring 12 goals in his 12 appearances for Newcastle United since he joined in March. We won the Division One title by eight points and we could see the sparkle of silverware for the first time in a generation, even if it was the second tier.

Selling Quinn and Kelly, which wasn't popular with the fans, Kevin proved he could make bold, difficult decisions, but he had the belief in what he was trying to achieve in the long term, and it paid off for him. A month later, he signed Peter Beardsley – his former Newcastle United strike partner – for his second stint at the club. The fans were thrilled with that move, but nobody would have predicted how good Beardo was going to be.

After the hysteria of the final game of the last season, we had belief and momentum going into our first season in the Premier League, which by then was only in its second season. But no one could have predicted what Andy Cole would do that 1993–94 season. I wasn't alone in doubting that he was good enough for the top level, but we were all wrong. Keegan knew what he was doing.

Despite signing Cole, we had a slow start to that season, losing to Spurs at home. Teddy Sheringham was up front, and he fizzed a shot wide in the first half and I thought to myself *I've never seen anyone hit the ball that hard.* It felt like a warning shot across the bows. It was one of those moments where the quality of the opposition we'd be facing really hit home. And then not long afterwards, Sheringham found the target, rounding Pavel Srnicek before celebrating by kneeling down right in front of me in the Milburn paddock. I remember thinking, *What a cocky b*stard* with both annoyance and respect. My dad said in the car on the way home, 'It's going to be a long, hard season.' We agreed that not getting relegated would constitute a brilliant season. But we weren't gutted about the Spurs result. We had our first taste of the big time. The next game, away to Coventry City, we got on the scoresheet, at least, even if it was a deflected free kick from Liam O'Brien. But then Srnicek got himself sent off after 34 minutes and we faced a barrage later in the game, which we couldn't withstand, Mick Harford securing a 2–1 win five minutes from time. The next game was a big one: Man United at Old Trafford and despite going behind in the first half, we showed some mettle and Andy Cole grabbed a second-half equaliser. We built on that with a home win against Everton, the start of an eight-game unbeaten run after that, with Andy Cole netting six times along the way. Cole and Beardsley proved to be an inspired partnership. Cole ended the season with 41 goals in 45 appearances and 34 in the Premier League. He even notched up 14 assists as well. His scoring record that season has only just been broken, almost 20 years later, by Erling Haaland.

Meanwhile, Beardsley didn't exactly take a back seat, scoring 24 goals himself including 21 in the Premier League (which would have very nearly won him the Premier League Golden Boot the season before) and providing 10 assists. People were saying he was past it when he came back to Newcastle United at 32 years old, but it might have been his best season. Fans still debate which was his best stint at Newcastle United, but with 61 goals in his 147 games (plus a handful of assists) the first time round, compared to 47 goals (and 35 assists) in his second stint of 129 games, it feels like the second stint edges it. He was one of the best players I've ever seen (maybe even the best), dancing around players, threading the ball through the eye of a needle and scoring some amazing goals on top of that. Keegan gave him a licence to just go and play his game and he did that, thrilling the whole of St James' Park. The football we played was always so positive, surging forward, and the fans lapped it up. Keegan had opened up the training ground to the supporters and thousands of us would turn up. You just can't imagine it these days, particularly with the kids lining the touchline and sometimes getting completely wiped out by a strong Brian Kilcline challenge. Everyone loved it. He'd completely united the city.

As a kid, I had a match report notebook that I'd fill out after every home game. It had space to write out the teams, the subs, the manager, the referee, everything. Maybe that's one of the reasons I remember the games I watched as a kid at St James' Park so well – because I relived the game and wrote it all down. And in the two weeks we'd wait for the next home game, I'd be reliving the previous game over and over in my head. And maybe it's something to do with not having mobile phones back then. You weren't distracted by this device that can tell you anything you want at the press of a button. We kids had to fill our own time in the early nineties!

Keegan had made us a serious team again. And all of a sudden we were buying people we'd actually heard of, like Ruel Fox (February 1994) and Darren Peacock (March 1994), both for well over £2 million each. And then, over the summer, Keegan signed a guy I'd seen play for Belgium at Italia 90: Philippe Albert. He didn't seem to play like any other central defender I'd ever seen. For a start, he didn't seem to think he was actually a defender. He was making all these runs high up the pitch, staying up after corners. He had a swagger about him and made a big impact both on the pitch and to the fans from the outset, helping to propel us to six straight wins at the beginning of the 1994–95 season. We were top of the table. And we smashed 10 goals past Royal Antwerp in our first two games of the UEFA Cup. We were in dreamland. Needless to say, it didn't last.

In November and December we started to draw or lose very winnable games. And then came the news that our number 9, my new hero, Andy Cole, was being sold to big rivals Man United in the biggest transfer deal in British history. It came as a massive shock to everyone. I was devastated. Suddenly Kevin Keegan was facing a group of fans on the steps outside St James' demanding to know why he sold Cole. 'When I came here a year and a bit ago our biggest rival was Southend United, now it's Man United. You have to trust me,' he answered. The fans were placated. We'd put our trust in Kevin Keegan so far, and he'd not only led us to the Premier League, but to Europe the season after. Have faith, we thought. And meanwhile Sir John Hall, our chairman, was promising to reinvest the money in the squad.

Here's what Kevin told me about what really happened leading up to Andy Cole being sold:

'He'd been tapped [up] by Man United. No matter what Coley says, his agent rang up and said he wanted to go and Coley wasn't training properly. The players saw it – I saw it. And if Man United come, I get it. We had two [away] games [in a row] and we stayed in Bournemouth. He just wasn't training properly and I just stopped the training and said, "If that's the best you can do, off you go," and he went. Never saw him again.

'We didn't play him at Wimbledon and we lost, but that was the end for him. We couldn't put up with that. He wanted to go – fine – he wasn't really training properly – you can't have that, so you have to make a decision, so we thought, *Who have they got that we like?* So we did a deal to take [Keith] Gillespie. I get it with Coley – Man United come and it's gonna turn your head, even if you're at Newcastle, great club thought it is, you know, it's Man United. And Paul Stretford, his agent ... told me they're interested. They really got in his head a bit I think.'

After a poor finish to the 1994–95 season, going winless for five games in April and early May, we just missed out on a UEFA Cup spot to Leeds. But, sixth place in your second season back in the top league? You'd have happily taken that before the season started.

In June 1995, the fans' faith in Keegan was repaid with the signing of Les Ferdinand from QPR. Keegan had probably written his name down on his little notepad (like he had with Andy Cole) after he watched Les single-handedly batter us at Loftus Road earlier on in the year, scoring twice in the first seven minutes. He went on to score 26 goals for QPR in all competitions and was an established England international. Andy Cole had left for £6 million (plus Keith Gillespie) and Les Ferdinand had come in, for £6 million. Everything seemed to be in order. But Keegan wasn't done yet. Wimbledon's Warren Barton became the most expensive defender in British history, moving in June 1995 in a £4 million deal. Shaka Hislop, Reading's player of the season in 1994–95 and one of the most talented young keepers around, joined us for just over £1.5 million. But it was the signing of David Ginola that got pulses racing (and certainly led to a few more female fans on the terraces at St James' Park). He was one of the most exciting players in Europe, so, all the top European sides were trying to sign him. Real Madrid. Barcelona. Bayern Munich. AC Milan. But he chose Newcastle United. No one could believe it. Plus, the guy looked like a movie star.

Keegan's ambitions and all the fans' hopes were being rewarded by the board. They'd forked out £14 million just in the summer alone. The 1995–96 season started and it was the first time that fans started believing not only that we could win the league, but also that we could be one of the big boys of Europe. St James' Park was having all sorts of modernisation work done to it at this point – it felt like the team was improving and so was the stadium around us.

The first game of the Premier League season saw us host Coventry and the atmosphere was at fever pitch. Our four new signings went straight into the starting line-up. The game started and it was end-to-end stuff. Shaka Hislop pulled off a fantastic save to deny Dion Dublin and then Coventry hit the post, but then Keith Gillespie, who already looked like he was going to give their left-back an afternoon to forget, sent in a cross and Rob Lee looped a powerful header over the keeper and into the far corner. Meanwhile, Ginola was just electrifying on the left. Peter Beardsley tucked a penalty away to make it 2–0, before Ferdinand's energy, pace and power were finally rewarded as he rounded the keeper, casually stroking the ball home from the edge of the penalty area on the far right. Game over.

Warren Barton summed it up well afterwards: 'I remember walking on to the pitch with Les Ferdinand and we couldn't believe what we were witnessing. We won 3–0 but it could have been 30–0. We were carried by our fans. We were invincible that day.'

Les was in unbelievable form, banging in 13 goals in the first 10 games, including a hat-trick against Wimbledon. Ginola was lighting up the league, setting up six goals and earning himself Player of the Month for August. By Christmas, we were 10 points clear at the top of the table. In February, we heard the news that Tino Asprilla had been signed. 'You've got to be kidding me! How the hell have we signed him? He's brilliant!' was my reaction, learning that one of the most exciting players on the planet was joining us. He was someone I knew already, being glued to the telly on Sundays watching *Football Italia* and Parma in particular. The season Asprilla joined us, he'd left a Parma team that included Buffon, Cannavaro, Zola, Brolin, Stoichkov and Pippo Inzaghi.

It was mental. He signed for another Newcastle United club record: £7 million. It was a statement buy and he was a statement player, from the moment he turned up in Newcastle during a raging blizzard wearing an oversized fur coat.

Everyone knows the story of the second half of the 1995–96 season, surrendering a 12-point lead with 15 matches to go. I thought it was as good as done and that we deserved to win it. I remember being out with my mates at about that point in the season and seeing the players around the Quayside a lot drinking. It happened a lot. But, being aware of this, Kevin decided that it would be a good idea to rein it in, so (the story goes) he says, in a team meeting, something along the lines of: 'We're never going to have a better chance to win the title. Stop all the drinking – let's knock it on the head, focus and get this one over the line.' So the players stopped going out on the lash, but then, amazingly, they started losing games every week. The rumour was that what made them brilliant was the team spirit fuelled by the team going out on the piss all the time together. It seemed that stopping drinking and behaving in a more professional manner was what killed our chances. Nothing could be more Newcastle if it tried.

The Man United game at Old Trafford on 4 March was a heavyweight clash. Whoever landed the decisive blow would win the title. It felt like we battered them and went out of the blocks at a hundred miles an hour, nearly scoring twice in the first five minutes. But Peter Schmeichel was like a man possessed – nothing could get past him. He saved 16 shots in that game and we lost 1–0 to an Eric Cantona volley. Even though it was still in

39

our hands, it felt like the momentum had shifted Man United's way. The whole city felt it. We were demoralised. Liverpool's turn-around at Anfield in April, seeing us squander a 3–2 lead to lose 4–3, proved to be the final nail in the coffin. Meanwhile, Man United just kept winning.

After all the high drama of the 1995–96 season, there were positives to reflect on. We had a hell of a squad and were playing some incredible football which had earned the team 'The Entertainers' tag. But seeing as we'd forked out £16 million in the previous season, I didn't imagine we'd be signing anyone quickly, let alone the best player in the world.

Signing Alan Shearer was seismic. He was the ultimate player for any Geordie – our local lad was England's number 9 – but until that point, he was seen as the one that got away. I'd just watched him become a national hero, taking us to the semi-final of Euro 96 and winning the Golden Boot, to go with his back-to-back Premier League Golden Boots. He could have signed for any club in the world. But he came back to his roots.

Al was kind enough to talk to me exclusively for this book and I asked him about the day he signed for Newcastle: 'It was one of the happiest days of my life. I actually signed more for Newcastle than I did for Kevin. I know Kevin had great persuasive powers and I know of his love for Newcastle and how much the club meant to him, the fans in particular. And the atmosphere he helped create – Kevin picked the club up and got it to a position where it could challenge at the top level and sign big players. He was a great talker, he wore his heart on his sleeve and he loved football. He was a great communicator and that's what he did really well, but it was really important for me that I wasn't going for the manager, I was going for the football club.'

Here's what Kevin said about that day to me: 'I met him [Alan] in Huddersfield in a little town house somewhere. I went with Terry. Man United had already talked with him and I said, "We want you to come. We're willing to make the offer." He'd already spoken to Sir Alex, and I was second in. But it was the lure of Newcastle for a Geordie. He said, "Look, I'm definitely going to sign but on one condition," and I thought, *Oh no, he's going to ask for more money … or for something massive like a house*, but he just said, "I want the number 9 shirt." I said, "You've got it." I didn't even think about it. And then Terry Mac in the car coming back, somewhere near Scotch Corner I think, he says "How are you going to tell Les [Ferdinand, our current number 9] about the shirt?" and I thought, *Oh my God, I'd never even thought about it – I've just taken his shirt off him*. Anyway, Les wasn't happy but he went along with it and that was it.

'The reason Alan came is because he's a Geordie and it was Newcastle United. We had a laugh about it and I told him, "You won't win anything up at Man United anyway." I think Man United won the league about eight times [while he was at Newcastle]. We didn't win anything up at Newcastle! But I think if you ask Alan truthfully, I don't think he regretted coming to Newcastle. The only thing is I didn't stay long after we signed him and I think that peeved him a bit. But he signed for the club not for me, but I get that. Players do come for managers and their style of play and you don't know what manager's going to come in next and what they're going to play like, but he did well there, breaking records.'

Then 63–year-old local lady Barbara Donaldson came up with one of the best remarks about Alan's homecoming, which really summed up the mood of the city: 'The morning he signed I went to get my pension. Normally they're a right grumpy lot but that day everybody in the queue had a smile like a Cheshire cat. If you'd put us in for the Olympic high jump that morning, we'd have set a world record.'

* * *

We didn't get off to the best start in the 1996–97 season, losing away at Everton and at Sheffield Wednesday in the third game of the season, but then we went on a run of seven successive victories, which sent us to the top of the table. And the seventh win was the sweetest because we were able to exorcise the demons by destroying Man United 5–0 at St James' Park. The second goal was a worldie from Ginola bending it into the top right corner from the edge of the box. Shearer, who was being pelted by the Man United fans for turning them down in favour of Newcastle United, latched on to a rebound and celebrated in front of the away fans. And the last of those goals was that outrageous chip from an ever-surging-forward Philippe Albert from well outside the penalty area, with Schmeichel just watching the ball sail over his head and into the back of the net. It was the icing on the cake and revenge for stealing the Premier League title from under our noses the previous season. As Alan Shearer said after the game:

'We've embarrassed them.' I felt that this had to be our year, if we can dispatch the champions like that, especially given that they'd come out on top in these heavyweight clashes recently.

Fast-forward just over two and a half months, though, and we'd only won one game in nine. Although we came back with a bang just after Christmas with a 7–1 demolition job of Spurs and a comfortable 3–0 home win against Leeds, nothing could have prepared us for what was about to follow. The resignation of Kevin Keegan.

It was a dark day. No one could quite believe it. We were fourth in the table, five points off the lead, just scored 10 goals in two big wins and were still in the UEFA Cup and FA Cup. So we fans didn't imagine it could be anything form-related. It had to be something going on behind the scenes. At the time, the statement Kevin released said:

'It was my decision and my decision alone to resign. I feel I have taken the club as far as I can and that it would be in the best interests of all concerned if I resigned now. I wish the club and everyone concerned with it all the best for the future.'

It was vague and we didn't really know what was going on.

Here's what Alan Shearer shared with me about hearing that news for the first time: '[It] was slightly surprising and disappointing considering he'd worked so hard to get me to the club. I know how hard he worked and how much he wanted me to come to Newcastle. Personally, the goals were flowing for me. I know we weren't top of the league but we were second or third – we'd just stuffed Spurs 7–1 and Leeds 3–0 at St James' when he made that decision. Something drastic must have gone on behind the scenes for him to do what he did but no one knew, so it was a big surprise and a big disappointment because he had the same sort of relationship with the players as he did with the fans – everyone loved him because of who and what he was.'

In his autobiography published in 1998, Kevin went a bit further, talking about how he wasn't enjoying the job and it had been the first time he'd experienced that. And then he gives us some insight into why he resigned:

'The people at the top of the club were preparing to float Newcastle United on the stock market and, as a rift grew behind the scenes, it had started to feel as if we were no longer all on the same wavelength.'

A lot of clubs floated on the London Stock Exchange after the formation of the Premier League in 1992. The stock market was making a lot of people rich then, and the broadcasting rights and sponsorship opportunities that came with Premier League status made football clubs a very attractive business prospect. To put that into figures, between 1995 and 1996, Man United and Tottenham Hotspur's share prices shot up by 336 per cent and 368 per cent respectively. Other clubs wanted a piece of the pie.

I asked Kevin about all this and what really happened leading up to his resignation after an epic road trip he and I took together (with his wife Jean) down to an event in Cornwall that he was appearing in and I was hosting. I've done a few events like that with Kevin over the years and we've become very friendly. Here's what he told me:

'I agreed another deal with [the club] maybe about a year into the job, but I hadn't signed it. No one had really pushed me for it, and I was being paid it so technically it was a contract. It was a 10-year one; that's what they wanted to do.

'So I was in my house one afternoon. I lived on Wynyard [the country house estate owned by Newcastle United chairman Sir John Hall] and bought the paddocks off him and about 70 acres because we raised horses and we'd rent them. I lived literally three or four hundred yards away from the main house [where Sir John lived]. And I got a phone call and learned that the club was going to be floated. And they got this guy in from the City to float the club and they'd got me to talk with the ice hockey people, the basketball people, the rugby people. Sir John was on about this total sports club ...'

Newcastle chairman Sir John Hall had bought the Newcastle Eagles basketball team, the Newcastle Falcons rugby team and the Durham Wasps ice hockey team. It was all part of his plan to turn Newcastle United into a 'sporting club', much like Barcelona. Here's Kevin again:

'I got really close to some of the [ice hockey] people who used to come and watch us train at Durham. We'd sit and have a bite to eat with them afterwards and chat. Well, when the guy from the City came, he said to Sir John, Shep [Freddy Shepherd] and Douglas [Douglas Hall, Sir John's son]: "Look, if you're going to float this club, you've got to get rid of the ice hockey, you've got to get rid of the basketball, you've got to get rid of the rugby, because they're all going to devalue it." So they just decided between themselves that they were going to get rid of them. When I went over to the big house ... Sir John didn't talk much, Freddie Fletcher [chief executive of the club] didn't talk much, which was unusual for him, Freddy Shepherd didn't talk much and neither did Douglas. This guy from the City, who'd only been with the club three or four months, he said, "Kevin, sit down, I'm going to be talking." I thought *Oh my God*. He said, "Look, there's your contract. Sign it now or go."

'And I looked at Sir John and the others and I said, "This guy doesn't know me from Adam but you people know me. I'm going."

'And I just walked back over to my house and I said to Jean, "Pack the bags, we're going." And we went to America because all hell was going to be let loose here. And that was it. That was the reason. Everything they said they were going to do and they got me to front, they didn't do. So when the money was put on the table and the guy said to him, "Hold on, that's going to cost you money having that team, taking that sport on board, it's going to be seen as a loss against the valuation of your float." And that's the truth. I felt like they just used me and of course I walked away from the contract. They didn't pay me any compensation at all. I just got my wages to the day I resigned and that was it. And that didn't bother me because it was my decision, but the guy from the City, *Oh my God*. I think it panicked them [that I hadn't signed my contract] because I think I was a part of that sale, you know, it was Newcastle United Football Club with me running it. They just thought he's not going to walk away from that 10-year contract, it was good money. They were generous with the wages, it wasn't a problem. And that was it.

'I don't regret leaving. They used me. They wanted me to help them build the club up and when they got to selling it, and some guy from the City says, "All the things you've promised people here – get rid of them, get rid of them." They could do that but, you know, I knew the guys, I knew their families, some of these guys had come from other countries, a couple of them were from America, ice hockey players and [the City guy said] just get rid of them as if they never counted. They would have done the same to me without even thinking about it if they thought that would help them. It was all about money. I don't care what they say, it was all about cashing in the club and getting the highest value in a float.'

At the time, when Kevin left, the fans were bereft. We'd been so close to winning something under Kevin but we couldn't get over the line. We had the players to do it. We definitely had the manager to do it. And for a time, the board bankrolled Kevin's ambitions even if they didn't agree with some of his moves. They trusted him. But that all fell apart with the potential to float the club. When that did happen, in what *The Independent* called 'a bonanza for the company's directors', joint chief executive Freddie Fletcher received £750,000 and the other joint chief executive, Mark Corbridge, who hadn't even been at the club for a year, walked away with £300,000. The finance director received £100,000. All 'in recognition of the part they have played in the recent development of Newcastle United'. Yes, some of the money raised through the flotation helped the club, but was that the motivation behind the decision to float? And did that money bring us any closer to winning anything? And was the personal payday all worth it at the cost of our talismanic leader?

Kevin's held in such high regard by all Geordies. I couldn't help but ask him what he'd think about a statue of him going up outside the ground one day, but I knew what he was going to say:

'You know better than anybody, Pete, that I don't want anything like that. My statue is the way they treat me. I don't want a statue and if they said, "Look, Kevin, we want to do one," I'd say, "No, thank you, I really don't want one." I get the Sir Bobby Robson thing, he was born there, but it's not something I want. I went to Alan's [statue unveiling in 2016] and I was late because we got stuck in traffic and Alan said, "You've missed my speech," and I joked, "Thank God for that. That's a plus!" I've got everything I want from Newcastle: the fact that people respect the time I was at the club and they know that we gave it everything we'd got and we tried lots of things that clubs wouldn't try because it was hard work, but we did it – the players did it. For me, every time I see a Geordie they're great with me and that's enough.'

CHAPTER 3

THE **BLACK** AND **WHITE KNIGHT**

Kevin Keegan was always going to be a hard act to follow but there was one man who had done it before. In his playing days, Kenny Dalglish had been signed to replace Keegan at Liverpool in 1977 and he had a stunning first season, scoring 31 times, including the winner against Club Brugge in the 1978 European Cup final. And now, here he was, taking the managerial reins after KK had so nearly steered us to glory. Dalglish was a proven winner – as a player he had 10 league titles (four at Celtic, six at Liverpool), 10 domestic cups, three European Cups and one Super Cup to his name, and as a manager, he'd won three league titles with Liverpool and had steered Blackburn both into the Premier League in 1991–92 and, then, against all odds, to the Premier League title in 1994–95. He was also the man who signed a promising 21-year-old striker by the name of Alan Shearer from Southampton in 1992. On paper, Dalglish was the man for the job.

Kenny's first half-season in charge (he joined in mid- January 1997) was a success: played 16, won 8, drew 6 and lost 2. Enough to secure second place in the Premier League and qualification to the Champions League second qualifying round. And that was a big deal because before then, only winning the league would earn you the right to compete in the Champions League. Unfortunately, though, our prolific strike partnership, who had racked up 49 goals between them the season before (the top two scorers in the league), was about to be broken up. Les Ferdinand, who was massively popular with the fans at St James' Park, was sold to Spurs for £6 million to balance the books. He'd scored 50 goals in 84 appearances and was the PFA Player of the Year for 1995–96. It was a shock to the system. Also, it proved to be a move that Les later admitted he regretted, telling Sky Sports he wanted to stay at Newcastle United for the rest of his career. And just as the deal was being done, we were dealt a mortal blow, with Shearer going down with a serious ankle injury in a pre-season game at Everton. It looked terrible but the repercussions were even more terrible. Shearer was out for over half the season. Meanwhile, fan favourites Lee Clark, Robbie Elliott, David Ginola and Peter Beardsley had all been sold over the summer of 1997 and it felt like both luck and judgement were in short supply.

I asked Alan Shearer about Kenny joining Newcastle and that first season in charge, and these were his thoughts:

'I knew Kenny extremely well and I thought success was almost guaranteed because I'd worked with him at Blackburn and we'd won the league there. But for us to sell Les Ferdinand six months after Kenny signed was a big mistake, whoever's decision it was. Maybe that was one of the reasons why Kevin left – because he felt as if he couldn't do things his own way. I was more than confident we could have done something with Kevin and was equally confident because of my relationship with Kenny that we could have won something with him. But, six months after Kenny signed, I was out for seven months, which was a disaster for me and more importantly for the football club because they'd bought players on the back of playing with me up front. After winning the Golden Boot the season before, I was more than confident of going out and winning it again, the form that we were in and I was in. We finished second that season but I'm convinced it could have been so much better for me, the football club, for everyone, and that without that injury, we would have challenged for the title. In the end, Kenny had to bring players in as cover that obviously weren't at their best any more – they were great lads, great professionals but weren't going to elevate us to where we wanted to go.'

The players Alan is referring to are the likes of John Barnes, Ian Rush and Stuart Pearce. They were all world-class players on their day, but these guys were now in the twilight of their careers and had been brought in as replacements for players like Les Ferdinand, Tino Asprilla and David Ginola. It just felt like a bit of a downgrade. (To be fair to Kenny, he also signed some absolute legends during his tenure – Gary Speed, Shay Given and Nobby Solano to name three).

The next season – 1997–98 – started brightly enough, with four wins in the first five games, but league form deserted us and we only won seven out of the remaining 34 games. We ended up in 13th place, but even that flattered us, finishing just four points above the drop. It was a different story in the FA Cup – we made it to the final at Wembley, which gave the fans something to cheer about. We showed some spirit after going down 1–0, hitting the post twice in the second half, before Anelka killed off the game for Arsenal. We went out of the Champions League in the group stage but not before an incredible 3–2 win over Barcelona (in a team that featured Luis Figo, Rivaldo and Luis Enrique) thanks to a sensational hat-trick from Tino Asprilla. Although Dalglish very nearly left Asprilla out of the starting eleven because he'd been having quite the time of it in South America before the match. Asprilla told *Four Four Two* magazine: 'I'd been away on international duty, but instead of going back to Newcastle I went to my ranch and had a party with lots of girls … Kenny Dalglish was furious.' What he got up to after that hat-trick is probably best left to the imagination, but given that his mantra was 'lots of s*x, no rules and pure life', you'll definitely have some idea. He was larger than life on the pitch and off it, and we Geordies absolutely loved the guy. In an interview with *La Gazzetta dello Sport* in January 2023 about what he was up to these days, he said: 'I'm excellent. I have a farm, I sell sugar cane to the Colombian government and through an advertising campaign, I sell condoms.'

Asprilla was sold back to Parma in January 1998 for £6 million and that left our front line looking ragged as Shearer wasn't back from injury yet. We were relying on Jon Dahl Tomasson, John Barnes and Temuri Ketsbaia, who'd been signed from AEK Athens over the summer. Ketsbaia became a cult hero at St James' Park, partly for his unbelievable celebration after scoring an injury-time winner against Bolton, throwing his shirt into the Gallowgate, trying to take his boots off, batting away Philippe Albert and then furiously booting the advertising hoardings. Alan Shearer revealed in the *Match of the Day* Top 10 podcast what happened in the lead-up to Ketsbaia coming on as sub and scoring that goal.

'Kenny took him outside a day before to say he was going to leave him out and you could see the steam coming off. We were all up there laughing and he chucked his phone. He couldn't chuck it at Kenny so he chucked it at the wall and his phone exploded. That was enough for the lads; you could hear the laughter of the lads. It was smashed to bits.'

That season, our joint top scorers were Alan Shearer and John Barnes with seven goals each, which goes some way to conveying the main problem we had. We scored 35 goals all season in the league. It felt like Dalglish's days were numbered and after two lacklustre draws at the start of the following season, chairman Freddy Shepherd wielded the axe.

Dutch legend Ruud Gullit took over in late August. He was young but he'd made the transition from player to manager impressively at Chelsea, steering them to the FA Cup in his first season, then as player/manager. It was their first big trophy in 26 years. When he was sacked, no one at Chelsea could believe it. They were second in the league, in the semi-finals of the League Cup and in the quarter-finals of the Cup Winners' Cup and then suddenly Chelsea chairman Ken Bates is talking in a press conference about being 'unable to match [Gullit's] demands' and announcing Gianluca Vialli as his replacement. It was all very strange.

Gullit only lasted just over a year at Newcastle United. Despite taking us to the FA Cup final in 1999, his approach just wasn't working for us. Two high-profile fallouts with fan favourites Rob Lee, whom he dropped, took the number 7 shirt away from and then refused to give a squad number to, and Shearer, who was infamously benched for the derby match against Sunderland on 25 August 1999, which we lost 2–1, did for Gullit. That was one of the worst nights I can remember being a United fan. It was absolutely bucketing down with rain and Sunderland pair Niall Quinn and Kevin Phillips tore us apart. All the while our own quality front two, Alan Shearer and Duncan Ferguson, were sitting on the subs bench with faces like thunder. The only positive thing to come from that night was that it proved to be the final straw for Gullit. It was our fourth loss in the first five games. He resigned three days later and it was a good job he did, because Shearer later admitted that he was on the brink of walking away from the club.

Our next manager was a stellar appointment. Bobby Robson was the guy who took England all the way to the World Cup semi-final at Italia 90, the tournament that I couldn't take my eyes off. He was the guy who'd managed Barcelona and won the double in the 1996–97 season – the Copa del Rey and the Cup Winners' Cup – as well as winning European League Manager of the Year. He'd won league titles in Holland and Portugal. And in England, he'd won the FA Cup and UEFA Cup. He was a winner. He was also a local lad, born in Sacriston, County Durham, just 15 miles south of Newcastle. He grew up a Newcastle United fan, and like me, his dad (who Bobby would often say 'bled black and white') took him to St James' Park on Saturdays growing up. To us fans, he was the perfect choice.

I talked to Bobby for a documentary I made at Century Radio celebrating his 75th birthday in 2008. I remember just before our chat, I met his PA (whom I'm still friends with now), telling me he didn't have much time today, which was a bit disappointing because I wanted to do a proper look back on his life sort of thing. But I went straight into our chat with a question about where Bobby had grown up in Sacriston and his dad working down the pits as a coal miner and Bobby really opened up. About an hour later, his PA came in and said, 'Bobby, don't forget you've got your dentist appointment!' and Bobby said, 'Oh, don't worry about that now!' We talked for another hour after that, at least, and I ended up coming back the next day and again the day after that. We talked about his early days 'playing football every night in the back street, playing headers against the wall', sometimes playing with a piece of coal or flint when they didn't have a football. He told me about growing up wanting to be a professional footballer and his memories of going to games at St James' Park. 'When I was 14, I used to be with my father at 1 o'clock outside the gates of Newcastle to be the first into the ground. All my heroes were Newcastle heroes: Joe Harvey and Jackie Milburn of course, who was my favourite player, and Albert Stubbins and Frank Brennan, Tommy Pearson, Charlie Crowe, Ernie Taylor, all those players. I remember those players like yesterday because I was a kid and they were my stars, my legends and I'll never forget about them. My father introduced me to the club and it's really been the love of my life.'

Bobby started playing local football for Langley Park Juniors and it wasn't long before his talent was spotted. He told me, again in 2008, that 'The North East was full of talent scouts, from all the clubs in the country, and when I was 17 I could have signed for Blackpool, Sheffield Wednesday or Lincoln City. I was already on schoolboy forms with Middlesbrough. Sunderland chased me, so did Newcastle and Fulham, so when I was 17 I had a big decision to make. The reason I signed for Fulham was because the manager was a fellow called Bill Dodgin and he travelled all the way up from London to see me and sat in my mother's sitting room and more or less would not leave until he'd persuaded my mother and father that Fulham was the club for their son. He also persuaded me – I liked him, he was a genial man and he made that effort to sign me.' Bill Dodgin's attitude of going the extra mile, looking people in the eye and treating people with respect while sticking by your convictions had a powerful impact on young Bobby.

Ironically Bobby's professional debut – aged just 17, in 1950 – was against Sheffield Wednesday, one of the clubs he'd turned down. He stayed at Fulham until 1955, when he signed for West Bromwich Albion for a then club record fee of £25,000. By the end of the 1957–58 season, he was the club's top scorer. At West Brom, he scored 61 goals for the club in 257 appearances before returning to Fulham in 1962. He eventually left Fulham and started working for Vancouver Royals in Canada before being offered the position of manager of Fulham in January 1968, midway through the season. The team were in dire straits, with 16 points from 24 matches in the league, and ultimately, Bobby couldn't stop them from being relegated to the Second Division in that first season, but the club stuck with him.

As manager of Fulham, right from the outset, Bobby showed he had an eye for a good young player, plucking forward Malcolm Macdonald from non-league outfit Tonbridge for £1,000. Macdonald would go on to Luton Town, Newcastle and Arsenal, becoming the top scorer in the First Division in 1975 and 1977 and scoring six times in 14 appearances for England. I spoke to Malcolm for the documentary I made to celebrate Bobby's 75th birthday, and he told me: 'He didn't just sign you as a footballer … he almost became a second father to you. He got to know you as a person, what made you tick, and he wanted to know how he could help you in any way. And he was absolutely marvellous. You felt that if there was any problem at all you could knock on his door.'

Macdonald spoke to me about what football meant to Sir Bobby, and his mindset as a manager from the start: 'He's got such a deep-rooted interest in the game of football and all of the people who make that game tick. He loves the game and the people that make it happen. So he loves everybody: the players, the directors, the coaches, the supporters, everyone, because he's the greatest enthusiast of them all. On the training ground, when it's a real cold winter's morning and the wind's howling a gale, there's Bobby, out there in his tracksuit, enthusing all the time with the players and encouraging them.'

By November in the following season, Fulham were sitting in eighth place in the Second Division, but the board wanted the club to be in the top three, mounting a challenge to bounce straight back up to the First Division. So Bobby was sacked, but the first he knew about it was when he drove past an *Evening Standard* placard announcing, 'Robson sacked'. Bobby actually thought it was a wind-up at first and tried to find another billboard or a copy of the newspaper. In his autobiography *Farewell but not Goodbye* (2005), he says '... there it was, splashed across the evening paper. Read all about it! I'd lost my job.'

Bobby had only been in management for eight months when he was sacked. 'I had no reputation, no credibility, no CV ... so who's going to employ me?' he told Gary Lineker in the BBC documentary *Just Call Me Bobby* in 2003, going on to add, 'I went on the dole. I didn't like it but I had to go on the dole – I had no money.' Six months later, Bobby caught a break and was hired as manager of Ipswich Town by chairman Johnny Cobbold which, to be fair, was a bit of a punt. As Bobby told Lineker, '... a lot of people had turned it down anyway so they were up the gum tree.'

Bobby was eternally grateful to 'Mr John', as he called him, for taking the chance on the rookie manager. Although they were worlds apart in some ways – Bobby, the son of a Durham miner, and Cobbold, the very eccentric Old Etonian descendant of the Duke of Devonshire and nephew of Prime Minister Harold Macmillan – Cobbold saw something in Bobby. It might have been something to do with the fact that Cobbold was 29 when he became Ipswich chairman (he'd become the youngest ever director of a football club at just 21), and Bobby was, at 35, very young at the time to be a football manager. Cobbold became 'like a second father' to Bobby and clearly the respect was mutual. Cobbold wasn't the only one to see that there was something about Bobby, though. Charlie Woods, a player Bobby inherited at Ipswich, who became a close friend and went on to become Bobby's chief scout at Newcastle, said, when first meeting Bobby: 'He walked through the door and there was something immediately that I thought was special. You could feel it.'

It wasn't an easy start at Ipswich, for Bobby, following a hard-line manager like Bill McGarry, which is something Bobby talks about in *Farewell but not Goodbye*. When Bill Baxter, one of the senior players in the Ipswich side, refused to follow one of Bobby's instructions during training, Bobby sent him home and dropped him for the next match. He also dropped their right-back Tommy Carroll, a friend of Baxter's, and after the team lost 4–2 at home to Leeds United, Bobby found the pair of them afterwards in the dressing room laughing. Bobby didn't blink and kept them out of the side for the next game, and that's when Carroll tore down the team sheet, shoved it in Bobby's face and told him exactly what he could do with his team. One more aggressive move later and Bobby was swinging a right hook at his right-back. Baxter joined in as did Bobby's number two, Cyril Lea, until players and other members of staff broke it up. Bobby later admitted to not being proud of his behaviour, but the gentlemanly approach just wouldn't have worked in that scenario. It was a trial by fire as a young manager back then and he had to fight to win the respect of his players.

It was a trial by fire on the financial front too. Here's Sir Bobby again talking to me in 2008: 'I ran the club on a pretty thin budget. We didn't have any money. In my day, as a football manager, there were two things that were spelled out very quickly to me by the board. One was, *Bobby, keep us in the First Division* and two, *Bobby, keep us in the black.* I learned to be, well, a financial wizard in a way. That's why I always said that at Ipswich the success of the club was the youth policy and the training and the coaching programme. We made schoolboys great players.'

Bobby famously signed very few players at Ipswich and guided them not only to European football but also the UEFA Cup (spanking a Saint-Étienne side that featured Michel Platini 7–2 over two legs on the way) by making the most of the lads that he had. In fact, in 14 years at Portman Road, Bobby only signed 14 players, which is incredible compared to these days when you might sign 14 players in 18 months. Bobby both blooded players from the Ipswich youth system and nurtured the squad players that he inherited, training them both up to greatness. Many of them, like Terry Butcher, George Burley, John Wark and Alan Brazil, became legends, repaying both Bobby and the club massively. His ways were admired up and down Britain by up-and-coming managers.

Here's my friend, former co-commentator and ex-Newcastle United manager Bobby Moncur, talking about Sir Bobby's early reputation as a manager:

'To any young manager, Bobby was like the king; he had so much knowledge. There are a lot of managers that have knowledge but won't let you have it; they keep their counsel to themselves, but with Sir Bobby, he loves the game of football, the people, the players, other managers and anything he could do to help, Bobby would do that. I remember as a young manager [up in Scotland], I was always looking to buy and sell and I phoned up Bobby one day and he said, "Why don't you come down here [to Ipswich] and we'll have a chat." So down I went, watching his players training, and he said, "The young lad there [the left-back] would do you a favour," and he came to us and did a good job. A couple of times, Bobby advised me where to find the type of player I wanted. Anybody would be off their head not to take advice from Bobby. He's a genuine fella, and when you're talking to Bobby, he looks you in the eye and tells you; there's no devious thing behind here, he's not telling me something that's not going to be right; it's spot on and it always is.'

In Sir Bobby's 14 years at Ipswich, he learned the trade of becoming a manager. For 10 of those seasons, he guided Ipswich into European competitions. 'I took little Ipswich to Barcelona, to Real Madrid, to Saint-Étienne, to Sparta Prague – you name it we went. We won the UEFA Cup in 1981 with a very good team and we knocked out some very good teams along the road,' he told me in one of our chats for the documentary in 2008. He led Ipswich to the Texaco Cup, the FA Cup, and for nine seasons on the trot Ipswich finished in the top six of the First Division. Outside Portman Road today is a life-sized statue of Bobby erected in 2002 in tribute to his phenomenal success and popularity.

His remarkable run with Ipswich led him to be offered the England job in 1982. The Ipswich chairman tried to tempt Bobby to stay with a 10-year contract at Portman Road, but the lure of the national side was too great. His first game was steeped in controversy though as he made a massive call, dropping captain Kevin Keegan from the side, something Kevin laughed about when I caught up with him in 2008. 'He's been a great man for football. I know he left me out of an England squad once but I've long since forgiven him for that!' It was a tough introduction to managing a national team, and they failed to qualify for the 1984 Euros, back when only the winners of the seven groups qualified. Things looked up at the 1986 World Cup in Mexico before going out in the quarter-finals in one of the most extraordinary games of football in history, featuring both the Hand of God and the Goal of the Century from Diego Maradona. What followed at Italia 90, though, was the stuff that dreams are made of. Here's Bobby, reminiscing to me back in 2008:

'I had a good team, it was as simple as that. We had a strong mentality, great players, some technical expertise, good team morale, good team spirit, very good teamwork, and everyone knew their job and their responsibility. We had wing play in John Barnes and Chris Waddle. I knew the importance of people who like to play wide and had speed and could accelerate past defenders. We played on the ground, exchanged passes, one-twos, give and gos, threading the ball through the gaps in the back four, and Lineker was quick, like lightning ... Peter [Beardsley] was quite quick but his brain was quicker. He saw the opening before it was there. Gascoigne came into the limelight and he was quite sensational, such a natural talent.'

But football can be cruel and the semi-final loss on penalties to Germany cut deep, but it was also a source of pride, as Bobby put it to me: 'If someone asked me what the worst misery was in my life, that would be it, the night we lost on penalties. But it was the greatest moment, in a way, of my life. If you'd have asked me, what were the greatest and worst times in my life, it would be that one match. My greatest feeling was the day we went out to play the semi-final and my greatest disappointment was at the end of the day when we lost.' I told him: 'The whole nation wept with you that night,' and he answered: 'But my bucket of tears was bigger than anybody else's, I'll tell you.'

Bobby became the manager of PSV Eindhoven straight after Italia 90. 'It was a proper club, a gentlemen's club, and it was run by top-notch people,' he told me. He won back-to-back Eredivisie (the Dutch First Division) titles but was surprisingly released because they didn't advance far enough in the European Cup. Bobby moved to Sporting Lisbon for two years after PSV, where he worked with a young Portuguese interpreter by the name of José Mourinho. He was up against an unpredictable club president, who sacked Bobby when the club was top of the table in December 1993, but their loss was their rivals Porto's gain, who snapped Bobby up, along with Mourinho, whom they hired as Bobby's assistant manager. Bobby's first silverware at Porto was the Taça de Portugal (the main domestic cup in Portugal) in 1994, ironically beating Sporting Lisbon in the final, before going on to win the Portuguese league twice. Bobby was affectionately nicknamed Bobby Five–O by the fans due to the number of times Porto won games by that scoreline. Bobby also got to know a precocious, football-crazy and fluent-in-English 16-year-old by the name of André Villas-Boas, who was living in Bobby's apartment block. Most people might have brushed him off, but

Bobby's encouragement, kindness and eye for talent led Villas-Boas to start work at Porto's observation department, which set him on the road to becoming a coach, something that Bobby later helped him achieve.

Barcelona came calling after Bobby's success with Porto, but it wasn't the first time they'd asked him to be their manager. They'd actually offered him a job when he was manager of Ipswich and later England, but he finally said yes at the third time of asking. He was at Barcelona for a year as manager before moving into the director of football position (a stipulation of his original contract), but in that one year, he won both the Cup Winners' Cup and the Copa del Rey. He also pointed the club's president to 19-year-old Brazilian forward Ronaldo, who joined them for a world record £13.5 million from PSV. He scored 47 goals in 49 games that season and the respect and admiration he had for Bobby was clear when he said, at a benefit auction in 2014 for the Bobby Robson Foundation: 'I have had a lot of managers in football but the difference between all of them and Sir Bobby was his humanity and the relationships he had with the players. He was always like a father to everyone.'

Bobby rejoined PSV in July 1998 as manager on a one-year deal before retiring. But as he told me, 'On the first Saturday of the next season, for the first time in 50 years, I wasn't working. I didn't like it – the season started and I wasn't in charge of a football club and I remember saying to my wife, Elsie, "I don't like this, Elsie, and I'm not going to go to the supermarket on a Saturday afternoon ever again!" Well, fortunately, or unhappily if you like, Ruud Gullit resigned and the job [at Newcastle] became available. I knew that I was in my sixties but I had a bright mind and I had great help and I didn't apply for the job, but I just kept reading the papers every day and soon it came out that I was one of the contenders. And then suddenly I got a call to say that they were very interested in talking to me about the position at Newcastle and would I be prepared to meet them in London. Well, I got to London in about two and a half minutes, and that was running!' he told me.

Then chairman Freddy Shepherd was kind enough to chat to me about that meeting with Bobby in London. 'It took two minutes to do the deal with him, two minutes. He wasn't interested in the deal – he was on his way to Newcastle in his mind. He wasn't interested in talking about money; all he wanted to know was who the players were, what was happening with Shearer and could he start tomorrow morning.'

Freddy wasn't exaggerating. Bobby told me himself: 'Straight away, I packed my bags, my suits, and my shirts and ties and I said to Elsie, "When I get something sorted out, I'll come back for you, but I'm on my way to Newcastle!" And I loved absolutely every minute of it. It was an absolute joy for me. We were in trouble, deep trouble – in fact I remember Freddy Shepherd saying to me at the time: "Bobby, you've got a very difficult job on your hands and I'm not so sure you can do it." I think everybody thought that year we were going down, not only into the First Division but into the Second Division. They thought we were in free fall. The second thing Freddy said to me was: "By the way, there's no money either – we had money but it's been spent, so you'll have to operate with what we've got." I said: "I've always done that anyway. I'll operate with the players that I have and we'll see what I can get."' I think if anything, that only made the job more enticing to Bobby. He proved what he could do at Ipswich when he didn't have a lot of cash to splash. You work with what you've got and try to make the best out of it.

At his official unveiling as Newcastle United manager, Bobby said: 'I thought Barcelona Football Club was quite big but I think this has just pipped it,' much to the fans' delight. He told me in 2008 that 'I wish he [my father] had been alive when I became manager of Newcastle United, I tell you; he would have done somersaults. For him, his son becoming manager of Newcastle United would have been unbelievable. He'd have been so proud of me.'

But there was little time for celebration at the time for the fans. We were winless in six league games, losing five of them, including the last game 5–1 at Old Trafford, with our former number 9 Andy Cole scoring four of them, just to make matters worse. We had a mountain to climb.

Here's what Alan Shearer told me about the day Bobby Robson arrived at Newcastle:

'My memory is incredibly positive of Bobby arriving. I'd spoken to some great players about how he operated and no one had a bad word to say, about who and what he was and how he treated players. That was the first thing that struck me really, the rapport that he was able to strike up straight away with the senior professionals who had basically been binned or sidelined under

Ruud Gullit. And I think he realised that he wasn't going to get anywhere without the senior professionals onside and that was his first job. And that's exactly what he did.'

Alan told me that that before the first game with Bobby in charge, he took a few of the senior players into his office and just spoke to them for half an hour, giving the confidence for them to get on the pitch and do what they could do. He was an incredible man manager and set the tone by being first in and last out to the training ground and the stadium. Meanwhile, on the pitch, Bobby went back to basics with a couple of wingers whipping the ball into Shearer in the middle. Rob Lee was reinstated to the starting eleven. And we Geordies lapped it up. It was in marked contrast to the overcomplicated 'sexy football' that Gullit wanted us to play.

Bobby's first game as Newcastle United manager was against Chelsea away before Sheffield Wednesday came to St James' Park the following week. Here's what Alan Shearer told me about Bobby's first two games in charge:

'Bobby only had a couple of days to set us up to train. He got Warren Barton to man-mark Gianfranco Zola and it very nearly worked. We got done 1–0 but we put up a good fight, but then of course, his second game, at home, we had a week to work for. He got everyone into shape, and just his mood and his atmosphere – he transformed the whole football club because of his positivity, experience and everything else that he brought with him. And everyone loved him and got on great with him. He just had this knack of making you like him and respect him. What was missing

from the football club was an atmosphere, a rapport and a togetherness, and then within a week that had all changed. It was back
to being happy and smiling. For me personally, I'd gone from rock
bottom to feeling ten foot tall again. To feeling the best forward
in the world again. To feeling as if I could score in every game
again, and that feeling had deserted me for a long time.'

Bobby's first game at St James' Park wasn't quite the deliri-
ous pandemonium of the Keegan homecoming, which was almost
like our Toon form of Beatlemania. There was excitement, and
lots of it, but there was also the sense that the captain was back
on the bridge of the ship. Everything would be OK now. Bobby's
here. And the first thing he did? Put Shearer back in the starting
line-up. Shearer responded like a man possessed, scoring a first-
half hat-trick and looking for all the world like he might end up
with a second-half hat-trick as well. In the history of the Premier
League, no one has ever scored a double hat-trick, but Shearer got
mighty close.*

Here's Alan Shearer again, chatting to me about Bobby's first
match at St James' Park as Newcastle United manager: 'That game
against Sheffield Wednesday has to be one of the greatest games
I played for Newcastle United. I was on the brink of having to
leave. I would have had to have left if Ruud had stayed ... And no

---

* In case you're wondering, five players have scored five in a game in the
Premier League. The other four were: Andy Cole in 1995 for Man United
in their 9–0 demolition of Ipswich, Jermain Defoe for Spurs in 2009 in
their 9–1 annihilation of Wigan, Dimitar Berbatov in Man United's 7–1
rout of Blackburn in 2010, and the last one the less said about that the
better. Let's just say it was Sergio Agüero.

one's scored more than five in a Premier League game still – but I'm sure that'll be broken soon and I'm surprised it hasn't gone this year [2023]. It was a great day for the football club because I think that was the day that everyone thought, *Right, we're back on the right track, we're not going to be relegated* and then it was all an upward curve from then.'

Danny Wilson was the unlucky chap in the dugout that day as manager of Sheffield Wednesday, and he told me for the 2008 documentary: 'It had to happen, didn't it, coming back to his beloved North East and getting a result like he did. Just after the game, he put his arm round me and said: "It only happens once in your career, son; don't let it get you down." And I haven't. It was great advice from a great manager.'

Before that home match against Sheffield Wednesday, we were rock bottom of the Premier League, but after just the first half we looked like a phoenix rising up out of the ashes. Bobby had brought pride, hope and joy back to St James' Park. We knew we wouldn't be fumbling around in a relegation battle under Bobby. We knew we wouldn't be challenging for titles anytime soon, but we had a decent foundation to launch from.

As soon as he was through the door, Bobby went about putting his unique stamp on the culture of the club. First and foremost was a return to the old-school values of hard work, decency, presentation and mutual respect. Bobby insisted on the whole squad eating together, and no one was allowed to leave until Bobby had finished eating. Everyone was quiet when Bobby was talking. You had your shirt pulled in and your socks pulled up, and the players were required to wear suits for the pre-match meeting at the Copthorne Hotel before leaving on the coach together for St James' Park. And when they got there, they'd greet the fans waiting outside the ground. They did the same at away matches too, signing autographs and giving people time. He gave so much of his time to other people.

Punctuality was a big deal, with latecomers to training told: 'If you were catching a train, the train's left the station and you're left on the platform.' He could be firm when he needed to be, but his sense of humour shone through. Ruud van Nistelrooy, whom he coached at PSV Eindhoven in 1998–99, remembered an incident in the PSV dressing room '… he drew Mickey Mouse on the board, then he said to the player, "You looked like him yesterday in the tackle," and all the players were laughing. And for that player, of course it was embarrassing … he can be hard but [has a] sense of humour as well, but it's the message behind it.' He got his message through and tailored his approach to suit the player.

In Bobby's first season, we finished 11th in the league – an incredible turnaround given the way the year started. And we closed the season out in style with a 4–2 win over Arsenal at St James' Park, with Shearer sending a thunderbolt of a free kick into the top corner – an amazing way to celebrate the 300th goal of his career (and 30th of the season). Bobby and Shearer led the team on a lap of honour, and everyone was smiling in the sun at St James' Park. It felt like we'd won a trophy, given the joyful scenes. We'd won our respect back.

Over the summer, we spent millions increasing the capacity of the Milburn Stand and the Sir John Hall Stand. St James' Park went from a 36,000 maximum attendance in 1999 to 52,000 in 2000. And Geordies had no trouble filling the seats – our average home attendance shot up to 51,309 in 2000–01, second only to Man United. The first home game of the season was against Derby County and the noise was deafening. Everything was going to plan, with 22-year-old new signing Carl Cort (Wimbledon and former England U-21 striker) scoring four minutes into the game after an inch-perfect cross from Nobby Solano. We ended deservedly winning the game 3–2 and after the match, Bobby said:

'We've had a good start at home and I think it was a fitting result for a fitting evening. It's been a marvellous emotional night for us, I mean what a stadium, what a public we've got here. At 3–1, I didn't even think the roof would stay on.'

That season, we finished 11th again – a decent finish for a period of rebuilding. And we weren't helped by some very unfortunate injuries, including Shearer's knee, which hadn't healed after an operation before Christmas, so he was ruled out from March for the remainder of the season. Like his injury-plagued 1997–98 season, Shearer scored just seven in all competitions and was still joint top scorer alongside Cort, who had showed promise, scoring seven in 15, but he was also out with hamstring problems for much of the season. Here's what Bobby had to say at the end of the season: 'We just had a horrific, horrendous season in terms of injuries. We lost Shearer for five months, [Kieron] Dyer for five months, [Kevin] Gallacher for three months, [Carl] Cort and

[Nikos] Dabizas were out, [Rob] Lee we lost towards the end of the season. It'll surprise you if I tell you that I never played my best team once in the whole season, so it wasn't ideal!'

It was in Bobby's third season that we really started to kick on. Shearer returned from injury after five months out, coming on for Shola Ameobi in the 75th minute in the Tyne–Wear derby to a rapturous reception. Even Shearer was moved, saying: 'I got up and warmed up and it sent a shiver down my spine.'

Club legend and adopted Geordie Rob Lee was given the honour of a testimonial against Athletic Bilbao at St James' Park before the start of the 2001–02 Premier League season, and he left the club in February 2002, having spent nearly a decade at the club, making 350 appearances and scoring 55 goals. There was more excitement at St James' Park when it was announced it was the chosen venue for the England World Cup qualifier against Albania on 5 September 2001 after the old Wembley was closed.

Shearer started the next league game, much to the travelling Geordies' joy, against Middlesbrough. And it was quite a comeback, scoring twice – the first, a penalty after Laurent Robert was fouled trying to go around Mark Schwarzer (who was sent off for the challenge), and the second, a finish he lashed home after some great work by Robert, who also had a blinding game, scoring his first goal for the club, this time rounding the keeper and slotting it in.

Then came a massive game: Man United at St James' Park and what a match that was to celebrate Bobby's 100th game in charge of the club. You couldn't have written the script better for that one.

It was breathless. We came out at 100 miles an hour and it paid off, winning a free kick after four minutes, which Robert stunningly curled into the top corner. I don't think anyone sat down for the whole game after that. Van Nistelrooy equalised after half an hour before Rob Lee got a bit lucky – not that anyone cared – with an effort that seemed to bounce past/over Barthez five minutes later. Dabizas scored after the break to make it 3–1, and it looked like it might be our day, but Man United pulled two back in two minutes, through Giggs and Veron. However, the momentum didn't shift the way we feared. Instead, Shearer's deflected shot at the Gallowgate End in the 82nd minute sent the Geordie faithful into dreamland. 'The roof nearly came off,' Shay Given said after the game. Shearer said, 'It was better than the 5–0 when Kevin was manager because I think that game had everything, seven great goals, two sides who were committed to try and win the game, going forward, leaving little gaps at the back … it doesn't get better than scoring the winner against Man United.' Bobby told the BBC: 'I can't survive too many games like this one!'

In November, Shearer scored his 100th goal for the club in a Worthington Cup win against Ipswich at St James' Park, putting him at ninth on the all-time Newcastle United goalscorers list, level with Peter Beardsley. The following month brought with it one of the biggest games in the 2001–02 season: the 3–1 win away at Arsenal, who went on to win the Premier League that year by seven points.

We'd come from behind after a Robert Pires strike early in the first half with a second-half near-post header from Andy

O'Brien. And then, five minutes from time, Kieron Dyer put Lauren Robert through with a beautiful outside of the boot pass but was brought down by a desperate lunge from Sol Campbell. Up stepped Alan Shearer who just blasted the pen straight down the middle to score (incredibly) his first goal at Highbury. Robert put the icing on the cake after he was put clean through to make it 3–1 with practically the last kick of the game. Bobby was pumping his fists on the touchline. Wenger was remonstrating with the officials. Not only had we beaten Arsenal at Highbury for the first time in years, it was also our first win in London in 30 attempts. And what made it taste even sweeter was that it sent us top of the table. Bobby talked after the game about how the dressing room was oddly quiet, with our players just shaking their heads, utterly shattered, wondering how on earth we'd pulled that off. We'd given it everything.

The next game, at Elland Road against Leeds, who were also flying high in the league, started where we'd left off. It was a seven-goal thriller, with us taking the lead through Bellamy before Leeds came back straight away through a Lee Bowyer finish. Two Leeds goals early in the second half made it 3–1 to Leeds, but we weren't done yet. A Robbie Elliott diving header followed by a Shearer pen following a handball set up a frantic finish. And then, in the final minute, Nobby Solano slid home past Nigel Martyn after being put through by a Dyer pass. Top of the table at Christmas! And a Manager of the Month award for Bobby.

Our title challenge ultimately faded, with losses to Chelsea, Man United, Arsenal and Liverpool, but it was a return to the

Entertainers era under Kevin Keegan. We were box office again. We scored 74 goals in the season, showed our resilience by coming from behind to win away from home at least five times. Shearer was on song with 27 goals for the season (including reaching the milestone of 200 Premier League goals, which he did against Charlton in April); Bellamy's pace was electric and he finished the season with 14 goals, Lomana LuaLua was backflipping all over the place; Nobby Solano was having an incredible season, scoring 12 and setting up an unbelievable 19 goals, as was new kid on the block Laurent Robert, with 10 goals and 16 assists in all competitions. We finished in fourth place, our best since 1997, and we qualified for the Champions League for only the second time.

After the final home game of the season, a 3–1 win against West Ham, Shearer was asked what Bobby's secret was with this team. He answered: 'Treating men like men and getting the best out of his players. It's a great example to any other manager to follow that man there through hard work.'

In the summer, Bobby was knighted for his services to football by the Prince of Wales. Somehow he'd managed to keep the news completely quiet, even from his wife Elsie, until the official announcement in the Queen's Birthday Honours. He told me in 2008 that 'to be given a knighthood is exceptionally special and for anybody who is good enough and lucky enough to be given a knighthood and to go through that ceremony – that thrill – has to be the second greatest day of your life … I'll never forget it.'

The awards were coming thick and fast for the newly invested Sir Bobby. He was awarded the freedom of the city of Newcastle upon Tyne the same year by the Lord Mayor, which he told me in 2008 'was as near and as dear to me as when I got my Sir, and you can't get much better than that. I felt a deep sense of pride, honour and I was full of humility and I couldn't believe really that it was happening to me.' That year, Bobby also received the UEFA President's Award, which recognises 'outstanding achievements, professional excellence and exemplary professional qualities'.

The 2002–03 season was even better than the one before but it was a patchy start to the season, with seven wins, six losses and a draw up to the end of November, including a 5–3 defeat at Old Trafford, thanks to a van Nistelrooy hat-trick, although Shearer did score his 100th Premier League goal for Newcastle United with a free kick that was hit so hard, it might still actually be travelling. He went one better in the next game, scoring one of the best goals I've ever seen in my life, and at such an important point in the game, losing 1–0 at home to Everton with four minutes to go. Richard Wright was having a blinder of a game, repelling everything that came at him like one of the Spartans in the film *300*, but then Shola Ameobi floated a long ball from Laurent Robert back towards Shearer and he caught a 25-yard volley so perfectly, and to hit a volley like that, that's always going to be dipping, and still manage to find the top corner is nothing short of miraculous. The commentator said: 'Cometh the hour, cometh the man,' and he was bang on. Not that I heard the commentator until *Match of the Day* later on. I was behind the goal going completely crazy. You knew it was in as soon as he struck it. That happened a lot with Shearer. As soon as he hit the ball, you knew it was going to end up in the net. Gary Speed said the same thing. 'As soon as I've sat down on the bench, the ball's come up in the air and even before it's hit his foot, I'm up off the bench, I'm on the pitch because I know it's going to be a goal.' Bobby called it 'one of the great strikes of modern football'. Here's what Shearer had to say about it in the Premier League's 'Shearer's Five Favourite Goals' compilation: 'You just take those shots on and hope that you catch it absolutely sweet. And I remember Bobby Robson saying at the end of the game that I'd probably never catch another ball as sweet as that in my career. And he was absolutely right because 99 times out of a 100, that shot ends up in the Gallowgate End.'

And the Gallowgate was still rocking when Bellamy squeezed in a shot via a deflection past Wright in the 89th minute. What a game.

We had a fantastic run in January and February and suddenly we were in a three-way title race with Man United and Arsenal. And on top of that, the Champions League provided no end of drama. After sailing through the qualifying round with a 5–0 aggregate win, we lost our first three matches of the group stage. But then we won the next two including beating Juventus at home. We had to win against Feyenoord away (who could also qualify with a win if Kiev lost), while hoping that Juventus beat Dynamo Kiev. It was all to play for and we went two up but were pegged back to 2–2 before Craig Bellamy managed to slide in an injury-time rebound off the keeper. 'Has there ever been a more dramatic night in the Champions League?' was commentator Jon Champion's line. It was an incredible turnaround – no team had

ever lost the first three games of the group stage and then qualified. Bobby had used every ounce of his European experience to
get the job done, including taking a few big gambles – Bellamy
had been out for three weeks with recurrent knee problems which
caused such concern that Bobby sought the advice of renowned
surgeon Richard Steadman in the States.

Our reward for that night was being drawn in the second
group stage alongside Barcelona, Inter and Bayer Leverkusen.
A group of death if ever I saw one. We gave it a good go, winning
both home and away against Leverkusen and drawing with Inter,
but Bellamy got himself sent off after about five minutes at home
to Inter, and both he and Shearer were injured for the game at the
Nou Camp, which wasn't ideal. But, playing against the best in
Europe and having them come to St James' was amazing. It felt
like the whole world was watching.

Our first game of the 2003–04 season was the third qualifying round of the Champions League against Partizan Belgrade.
We beat them 1–0 away from home, so everyone felt that the hard
part had been done. But then, they scored at St James' Park to take
it to extra time. Penalties followed and it was one of the weirdest
shoot-outs I've ever seen. Not only did Shearer not score, which
was pretty much unheard of, but the next five penalties were saved
as well. They went through after Aaron Hughes sent the ball sailing over the bar and it was a shambolic end to a catastrophic night.
At that moment, it felt like the whole Premier League season before
had been a complete waste of time. As it turned out, we dropped
into the UEFA Cup and ended up going on a great run, beating

Mallorca and PSV Eindhoven along the way to the semi-final. There we faced Marseille, on 6 May 2004, but the game came along at a difficult time, when we found ourselves without Bellamy, Jenas, Dyer and Bowyer. A 0–0 draw at St James' Park wasn't enough and a Didier Drogba double did for us at the Stade Vélodrome.

In the league, we had an underwhelming start, drawing with Leeds and then leading Man United at half-time at St James' Park, only for van Nistelrooy and Scholes to score in the second half and win the game. Alex Ferguson was watching from the Milburn stand, after he'd been sent off by Uriah Rennie after a scuffle with the fourth official early on. By October we'd gone six games without a win, the last of which was a 3–2 defeat to Arsenal, a week after their incredible game at Old Trafford, where Vieira was controversially sent off and van Nistelrooy smashed a last-minute penalty against the bar and was then confronted by an absolutely seething Martin Keown. If he'd scored, that team would never have been known as the Invincibles. Such fine margins in this game!

But Bobby turned things around, winning the next four games on the bounce to move us into the top half of the table and earn himself the Premier League's Manager of the Month award for October. By the New Year we were in seventh and, after a good run in February, we were up to fourth. I remember the last home game of the season at St James'. We were fifth in the table, only separated from fourth-placed Liverpool on goals scored. It was three days after our UEFA Cup semi-final defeat in Marseille and we could only manage a 1–1 draw against a struggling Wolves side that were facing relegation. Wolves equalised 20 minutes from time after Lee Bowyer had put us ahead. To make things worse Alan Shearer missed a late penalty and the full-time whistle was met with certain sections of the ground booing and jeering. It felt like a massive missed opportunity and severely dented our Champions League hopes. When Bobby led the players out for the traditional lap of honour after the final home game of the season, many of the supporters had already gone home. Yeah, we'd just lost a big semi-final in Europe and yes we should have won the game on the day, but we were still fifth in the league and it felt like we'd been spoiled with a couple of good seasons and we didn't know how good we had it. I often think back to this match and swear to myself that I'll never take success for granted again at Newcastle United. This feels particularly relevant now (in 2023) as we continue on this journey with Eddie Howe.

Over the summer, we signed James Milner for £5 million from Leeds, Patrick Kluivert from Barcelona on a free transfer (he'd been released after six years, having scored 124 goals in 249 appearances), Nicky Butt from Man United for £2.5 million, Charles N'Zogbia from Le Havre for just £250,000, and Stephen Carr from Spurs for £2 million.

On 30 August 2004, amid rumours of discontent in the dressing room, a winless start to the season and growing criticism among some fans, Freddy Shepherd sacked Sir Bobby Robson.

Here's the statement the club released:

'After a disappointing start to the Barclays Premiership season the directors of Newcastle United have informed Sir Bobby Robson that they have decided he is to be replaced as team manager.

The directors of Newcastle wish to place on record their thanks for the way in which Sir Bobby has worked tirelessly over the past five years to try to bring success to the club.'

It was a decision greeted with disbelief among the vast majority of us.

In 2008, Freddy Shepherd admitted to me that it was one of the toughest decisions he's ever had to make. 'It wasn't a unanimous board decision – although I was chairman, it wasn't unanimous,' he said to me before adding, 'Without a doubt, I think he could have gone on a bit longer. I think he was on the right track. I think he had a poor start to the season and perhaps certain people overreacted.'

Bobby responded to the club's announcement at the time, telling the press he was 'massively disappointed not to be able to finish the job I came here to do'. A month later, he admitted to Des Lynam on BBC Radio 5 Live that, 'It was a shock to be sacked. I was bewildered.' In our chats in 2008, Bobby reflected on his time at the club: 'I remember saying to my wife, "Well, I'll probably last two years, football being what it is, two years and I'll get kicked out, for some reason or other," but I stayed five, put the club in the top echelon of the league, for sure. I say this with a certain amount of conviction and pride and forcefulness because it wasn't easy. I took over an ailing side and in the last three years we finished third, fourth and fifth. And that's where we have to be.'

So what really went wrong for Bobby?

A growing section of fans were expressing their discontent – that much was clear at St James' Park. But so were some of his players. Behind the scenes, in the week before his sacking, everything had unravelled. According to Bob Harris, two senior players had gone to see chairman Freddy Shepherd to tell him Sir Bobby had lost the dressing room. Shepherd was shown a picture taken by a local photographer of one of the senior players putting two fingers up behind Sir Bobby's back. Bob Harris tells us that Shepherd paid off the photographer to make sure the photo didn't appear and damage Bobby's reputation.

Kieron Dyer had refused to play on the right wing against Middlesbrough on the opening day of the 2004–05 season. But even after the story appeared in the paper with a picture of what looked like an argument between them, Bobby protected Dyer, telling the press the report of an altercation was 'utter rubbish' before explaining that his decision to bench Dyer was down to 'hamstring problems and he hasn't had the best of preparation'.

To be fair, the whole build-up to that Middlesbrough game was really strange. There had been an outbreak of conjunctivitis among at least five players, so the club approached the Premier League authorities to defer the game on medical grounds, as it was believed a number of other players were incubating the virus and could spread it to the Middlesbrough team. The request was denied, but the whole situation meant that Newcastle players had a massively disrupted week, with the training ground shut down and each player getting changed in their cars. It wasn't exactly ideal preparation.

And then, the drama going on before the game was matched by the drama on show at the Riverside. Firstly, we were forced to field a makeshift back four, with Robbie Elliott (in his first game for two years) playing as centre-back. And with barely a minute gone by, Elliott got away with what looked suspiciously like a handball from a Hasselbaink header in the area. Then, with only 14 minutes on the clock, and against the run of play, Chris Riggott let a pass somehow slip under his foot, which Bellamy was on like a flash and went round Mark Schwarzer with a neat side-step. Kieron Dyer, meanwhile, found himself on the bench, with the newly signed James Milner (then a fresh-faced 18-year-old) starting on the right. But then, in the 68th minute, Dyer came on for Milner. On the right wing. Five minutes later, Hasselbaink squared a ball into the area to find Downing, who just about put it past Shay Given. But then, we were given a lifeline in the 83rd minute, when young Shola Ameobi, who'd just come on, was tripped near the edge of the box and Shearer stepped up to smash the penalty into the roof of the net. You'd have bitten your arm off for a 2–1 win the day before the game. And it could have got even better but Jenas, who was having a blinder of a game to that point, missed a sitter. Bobby was holding his head in his hands on the touchline. And then, in the 90th minute, Dyer slips (actually to call it a slip sells it a bit short: it's more of a full-on face plant, which Dyer later acknowledged), Zenden whips in a cross and Jimmy Floyd Hasselbaink somehow bundles in an equaliser at the far post with a combination of head, hand and hope. I was in the away end that day and getting pelted with coins from the Boro fans above. Not pennies though – £1 and £2 coins that were fairly hefty. My mate and I got on our hands and knees and managed to collect about eight quid in total, which paid for our beers. What a result that was, at least.

Just a few days later, on 20 August 2004, came the news that Jonathan Woodgate was being sold to Real Madrid for £13.4 million, which came as a surprise to everyone, given that he'd been out through injury since April. According to Bobby's close friend Bob Harris, Bobby was 'bypassed' in that sale, as he had been when Gary Speed left for Bolton the month before.

Three games later and we hadn't registered a win – that's when the board made their move. On paper, it was a bad start to the season, not a catastrophic one. I'm still amazed there was any discontentment among any of our fans. The ones moaning must look back and think they should have been more appreciative of what Bobby had achieved in the time he was with us. He'd made us compete at the highest level again. He'd given the senior players like Shearer respect, faith and confidence to go and do what they did best and they rewarded him and the fans in spades. Discussing Bobby's impact at the club, Alan Shearer summed it up to me:

'Not only did he change my fortunes around; he certainly changed Newcastle's around. And in the space of two or three years, rather than fighting relegation, we were playing Champions League football, which is great credit to the man himself for how he handles players and tough situations ... Bobby took us to nights in Rotterdam and Milan and all of these incredible, iconic European grounds. That night in Milan [11 March 2003, where Newcastle drew 2–2 in a fantastic performance] will live with me forever because I always look back at 14,000 travelling Geordies behind that goal. For me to score in both halves, the second in front of the Geordies – my God the noise that night, hearing them going berserk, was an incredible feeling. In hindsight, of course it was a mistake to let Bobby go, from where he took us to where he elevated us to.'

Bobby had established a sense of calm decorum at the club, insisting that players arrive to training on time. You'd hear stories about him making youth players take their flashy cars back that they'd been driving to the training ground. He didn't want his young players getting cocky and ahead of their station. Bobby was also brilliant at making tactical substitutions when a game wasn't going our way, sometimes replacing three players at a time (which was pretty unheard of back then) to totally freshen up the team.

But more than anything else, Bobby was an incredible man manager. He could make players feel like a million dollars – you only have to see how Shearer responded when he was restored to the starting line-up after Bobby took over. Bobby had the ability to read a situation perfectly and know exactly how to handle it, sometimes dishing out encouragement and other times giving people the kick up the bum they needed. Kieron Dyer recalls a dressing-room incident in his book, *Old Too Soon, Smart Too Late*, when Craig Bellamy was pulled off when Newcastle United were winning as Bobby was keen to save Bellamy's legs. Bellamy wasn't happy and started complaining about how he was always the first one to be subbed, swearing loudly in the dressing room. After repeated warnings from Bobby, the first of which was, 'Will you shut up,' and the second, 'I'll squash you like an ant, son,' Bellamy still persisted.

So Bobby said to him: 'Who are you? Ronaldo, Romario, Stoichkov, Hagi, Guardiola, Luis Enrique, Gascoigne: these are the people I deal with. And who are you?'

Dyer says the whole dressing room went quiet after that. And then Bellamy looks over to Dyer and says: 'He's got a point, hasn't he?' In his official biography, *Craig Bellamy: GoodFella*, Bellamy called Bobby 'the best manager I've ever worked with' and talked about how he expertly handled a bust-up between Bellamy and assistant manager John Carver. Bellamy explained that he turned up to training before Carver on the day of a UEFA Cup match away at Real Mallorca. Because he felt like coaches should be there before the players, Bellamy deliberately parked his car in Carver's allocated space – something Bellamy knew would really annoy him. It all kicked off between them at the departure lounge at Newcastle Airport. When Bobby saw what was happening, he was furious with Carver, asking him what the hell he was doing and telling him to get on the plane. Meanwhile, Bellamy had lost control and was repeating, 'I'm not going. I'm not getting on the plane.' Bobby put his arm round Bellamy and said, 'Walk with me, son,' before asking him how his wife and kids were and how they were doing at school. While he answered Bobby's questions, he didn't even realise where he was going. 'The next thing I knew I was on the plane. I was thinking, *How the f*****g hell have I ended up here?!*' Bellamy explained, before adding, 'If he told me straight that I had to get on the plane, if he'd ordered me to get on, I wouldn't have done it.' In the game itself, Bellamy came off the bench against Real Mallorca, scored with basically his first touch, and Newcastle United won 3–0. Bobby was masterful at knowing what to say and when.

Bobby genuinely knew all of his players and what they each needed to hear, as Alan Shearer told me:

'As a man manager, Bobby was a genius. From the moment he walked in the door to the moment he left he knew how to make you tick, whether you were a 17-year-old kid or a 35-year-old senior pro, whether you were on 500 quid a week or 50 grand a week. He knew how to get the best out of you. I know it was tough for him towards the end but that was his greatest strength, his ability to manage people. He was incredible at that. He had a knack of making you respect him, making you like him and wanting to go out and smash that shirt for him. That was his greatest asset.'

We'd got ahead of ourselves, assuming that Champions League football would come every season. But I guess we'd had a two-year taster of club football at the highest level, and with that everyone's expectations rise. Pundits make a lot of the age divide between Bobby and his young squad, and maybe there is some merit in that. The average age of the starting eleven was 28.6 in 1999–2000, and by 2002–03 it was 23.5. He did have some challenging young players to manage, there's no doubt about that. He was in an era where every single player would drive a fancy car to the training ground; Kieron Dyer left his £65,000 earring behind in the dressing room at an away game and begged Bobby to turn the team bus around. Bobby couldn't quite believe the things he had to contend with, but it didn't tarnish his reputation as one of the greatest man managers in football history.

It's hard to point a finger at any one thing. Some fans weren't happy, some of the players weren't happy; Bobby was doing his best but there was talk that he was being sidelined for major transfer decisions. The club had refused to extend Bobby's contract beyond the end of the 2004–05 season, which perhaps gives an indication about how the club felt at board level. It was also a decision Bobby was disappointed by and didn't agree with. So the four major components of the club – players, fans, manager/coaching staff and the owner/board – were all unhappy. Something had to give and ultimately it was Bobby who paid the price.

But what would follow that decision? Utter shite for years.

CHAPTER **4**

CHANGING OF THE **GUARD**

Graeme Souness was the man Freddy Shepherd appointed, on 13 September 2004, to pick up the pieces a week after Bobby Robson was sacked. Souness had a bright start, going unbeaten in his first 10 games but then just one win in the next 10 followed and we hobbled to the end of the season in 14th place, well clear of relegation but some way short of the fifth, third and fourth places Bobby had guided us to. We felt like we were taking a big backward step. And after a poor start to the 2005–06 campaign, Souness was sacked in February 2006. He'd lasted just under 17 months, and the less said about that period the better. The few things that do come to mind are real low points – a massive falling-out with Craig Bellamy that led to him being loaned out to Celtic, and then Lee Bowyer and Kieron Dyer having a scrap on the pitch during the 3–0 defeat to Aston Villa at St James' Park and both getting sent off. That was a dark day. And under Souness, we were in a dark place.

Meanwhile, the previous summer, I'd started doing work experience at ITV Tyne Tees (the ITV franchise station for North East England) after I graduated from university. I was working on a programme called *Pub Stories* produced by Ian Lennox and starring actor Glenn McCrory, who had been the IBF cruiserweight boxing world champion in 1989–90. Glenn is a bit of a local hero for bringing a world title back to the North East and someone I know pretty well these days. The programme was about people chatting in a pub, and I just helped in the background as a runner. During breaks in filming, we'd all get chatting about football and I remember Ian telling me, 'You know loads about football for a young lad.' And to be fair, he was right – I was a bit of a sports nerd, reading back over the history books about this team and that. So Ian asked me if I wanted to see the sports department at Tyne Tees TV and I met Roger Thames, who was then head of sports there. We had a chat and he offered me a part-time job logging tapes and doing admin work. It was a foot in the door.

Then, a job advertisement came up to be an on-screen reporter and I was thinking about going for it, but Roger advised me that I needed some broadcasting experience on the CV first, so suggested I do a bit of radio. That led me to volunteer at my local hospital, which had its own hospital/community radio station, Radio Tyneside. I did quite a few shifts there, which helped me on to a job at Metro Radio, one of the local radio stations in Newcastle. And Metro had the rights to broadcast the commentary from Newcastle United games. When I started at Metro, I was helping out on match days and doing the odd interview in the players' tunnel, stuff like that. It was a dream come true to be honest, being at St James' Park in an official capacity and getting paid for it.

I got my first break as a commentator when the wife of the regular commentator – Justin Lockwood (who still does the on-pitch kick the ball through the hoop fun and games at half-time at St James' Park) – went into labour so he couldn't make the game the next day, which was against Portsmouth at Fratton Park. It was 1 October 2005. I suppose the bosses at Metro looked around for another 'higher profile' commentator, but at that kind of short notice they had no luck. But being a young lad keen to grab any opportunity that came up, I said, 'I'll do it, I'll do it!' and they gave me a shot.

I was meant to be commentating with Mick Martin, a regular on the radio and a former Newcastle United midfielder in the late seventies and early eighties, but it just so happened that he couldn't make the game either. So I ended up doing the game with a Scottish ex-Everton and ex-Newcastle United player called Jim Pearson. In our first conversation, he told me he'd never commentated before and that he'd need a bit of a guiding hand. Looking at me for reassurance, I told him that I'd never done it before either, so we both stared at each other and said, 'Oh shit!' at the same time. But, in a funny way, that revelation made me less nervous and we limped through the game together. I remember being really anxious about what to do if one of the teams scored. It sounds silly but how you react to goals is what separates the good commentators from the really bad ones. It's the goal commentaries that end up in the highlights segments and news bulletins throughout the rest of the weekend. In short, the goals are what you're judged on as a commentator, so I was worried about what I might say or do and how I'd say it. I'd tried to prepare a few lines beforehand that I could rely on when the inevitable goal came along, which in this case it never did. I think it was the only time in my life I'd been that happy at a 0–0 scoreline, an uneventful match and no big moments! It was the perfect, gentle introduction to football commentary.

Luckily, the bosses were quite happy with my performance. After that, Justin Lockwood came back to work, but there were only a few games of the season left and he was dealing with a newborn baby at home, so he asked me if I wanted to cover the matches alongside Mick Martin. I said a resounding yes. And I absolutely loved that job. I'll be forever grateful to Justin for giving me that opportunity as it provided the launch pad to everything else. I also learned a lot working alongside Mick Martin. Mick was a great guy who made me realise that I needed to know a lot more about the history of the club. I went about researching the players and managers from before I'd started going to the matches. The only downside to Mick was that he was a terrible passenger in the car. I'd be driving to an away game and he'd be drifting off to sleep, then he'd suddenly wake up and go mental that I'd driven too close to the edge of the motorway or something. It always made me laugh and eventually he'd start laughing, too.

I ended up with the nickname 'Shaky' soon after I started, because I'd go into the press box, introducing myself and shaking everyone's hand. Maybe the name also rang true because I was just a kid, really, barely over 20, and was a bit nervous. Looking back, I definitely had imposter syndrome going on because I'd gone from making cups of tea and photocopying to commentating on Newcastle United games and even interviewing players. The first player I interviewed in the tunnel was Alan Shearer, believe it or not, and the microphone was literally shaking in my hand then. But even though my questions were probably terrible, Alan really looked after me, giving me great answers and probably answering the questions I should have asked rather than the ones I did actually ask. He went out of his way to help and encourage me.

After I'd started at Metro Radio, I would always take tips and advice from other members of the North East press pack who really looked after me. There are too many to mention by name but you all know who you are. I learned quickly that you always needed to prepare notes – a few choice nuggets basically – on all of the players. But I also realised that for Newcastle United, most of the information was already in my head. I was such a massive fan and knew everything about the current squad, where they signed from and how many assists and appearances they had already. I was learning more and more about the history of the club, former seasons, former players, that sort of thing, that I didn't need to rely massively on my notes. It just came out of me. All the work I did went into the opposition. It's the same now for Newcastle United games on Sky. I don't need to research anything specifically for us, but I do for the opposition or if I'm covering a game not involving Newcastle United. To be fair, back then when I was working on Metro Radio, I probably didn't need to do as much work on the opposition, because the beauty of local radio stations is that nobody really cared much about whoever we were playing!

On my commentary journey, the best thing that happened to me was at another Portsmouth game, but this one was at St James' on 25 October 2006 in the Carling Cup. Glenn Roeder, the former Newcastle United captain in the mid-1980s, who'd played nearly 200 games for the club, had been given the reins as caretaker manager in May. He had already been part of the coaching staff set-up at the time at Newcastle, working as youth development manager.

All my commentary prep work on Portsmouth and the stats I'd put together were on lined paper, but we were sitting in these seats without any cover overhead. And then it absolutely bucketed it down in proper Newcastle fashion. So all my paper just turned to mush. Nothing was legible, so I had no choice but to chuck it. Suddenly I've got nothing to work with and I had to wing it. It went … all right, I thought. And then, the boss at Metro Radio wandered over to me the next day. 'I caught you on the radio last night,' he started, and I was thinking, *Oh no* …, but then he said, 'You were fantastic!' So after that, I decided not to come in with stats and notes and all that. My plan was to turn up and just *be me*. And that meant being massively passionate about Newcastle United. I suppose my style was a bit like Fanzone or like some kind of early YouTuber. When Newcastle United scored, I didn't try and temper my reaction. I went absolutely mental, as I would do at the game anyway. And people seemed to respond really well to that energy and joy. Some of my commentary clips ended up on YouTube (it was quite young then) with headings like 'Local commentator goes crazy'. Someone put the highlights footage from *Match of the Day* with my commentary over the top, and that went down well. It was mad seeing that clip and it really made me laugh.

Roeder had a bumpy start as manager, as he didn't have the UEFA Pro Licence that you need to manage a club in the Premier League. He was eventually awarded special dispensation on medical grounds after suffering from a brain tumour in 2003, which prevented him from going on the UEFA course he'd enrolled in while manager of West Ham. But the League Managers Association (LMA) was furious with that decision, accusing Newcastle chairman Freddy Shepherd of attempting to circumvent the rules. But with Alan Shearer appointed assistant manager (he'd already been working as player/coach), the managerial combination seemed to work well from the outset. We won five of our next six games, and despite losing the next four games after that, we finished really strongly, going unbeaten in the last six matches and winning five of them.

There had been some unfortunate news in mid-April, though. After helping us thrash Sunderland 4–1 at the Stadium of Light with a penalty that he characteristically smashed home, Shearer limped off with what looked like a knee problem. It was the last time he'd play in a Newcastle United shirt. He'd achieved legendary status some time before then, and although he was still going to be heavily involved at the club, it was the end of an era. The local boy turned Premier League record goalscorer, England captain and Golden Boot winner at Euro 96 had finally hung up his boots.

That season, we finished in seventh place and you would have bitten someone's arm off to take that back in early February. Freddy Shepherd seemed happy enough to reward Roeder with a two-year permanent deal. And that seventh-place finish meant we qualified for Europe. We'd somehow battled our way into the preliminary rounds of the UEFA Cup and also gained a place in possibly the most Mickey Mouse trophy in the history of European football: the Intertoto Cup. However, Roeder deserved a lot of credit for the way he'd turned things around. I always really liked Glenn as a person. He was a kind man with time for everyone and he understood the club and the supporters. He was probably never going to be the answer in the long term, but his appointment had definitely lifted the place, and the season ended with an air of positivity on the terraces.

The summer of 2006 saw us sign a genuinely exciting young player: 21-year-old Obafemi Martins from Inter Milan for just over £10 million. He'd become the first teenager to score in three consecutive Champions League seasons, looked like he could outsprint 100-metre Olympic gold-medal winners and was being touted as a possible long-term replacement for Big Al. He inherited the number 9 shirt and thus became my new hero.

Martins banged in 17 goals in his first season, but it was an inconsistent season at best for the club, not helped by a terrible injury crisis. In the end we finished in 13th place, but only five points clear of the relegation dogfight and Roeder resigned a week before the end of the season. Slightly farcically, we ended up winning the Intertoto Cup, but the whole thing was a joke really. We entered in the third round of the Intertoto Cup, won that over two legs and then qualified for the UEFA Cup (along with 10 other teams qualifying via the Intertoto Cup). The winner of the Intertoto Cup was the one of those 11 teams that advanced the furthest into the UEFA Cup. So because we were the only Intertoto entrants who had made it through the UEFA Cup group stage, we were 'awarded' the cup on 16 December 2006, although as we were still in the UEFA Cup, the whole thing felt very strange. Glenn Roeder said, 'We will be very happy to receive it. It would be disrespectful to consider it a lesser tournament, as some managers do.' But I'm not sure it's actually even a tournament, is it?!

In early 2007, I heard the news that Metro Radio had decided to become more of a music channel and were stepping away from commentating on live games, so I suddenly found myself out of a job. I was absolutely heartbroken because I'd just started to get into commentary properly and I knew I was improving. I wasn't ready to give it all up and go back to reading news bulletins every hour. But then, I caught another break. Century Radio, Metro's main rival station, were taking on the rights to the commentary for Newcastle United games, so I got in touch directly to ask if they'd be interested in hiring me. I wasn't sure if I'd even get a response but they emailed back to say that they'd heard me on Metro, liked my stuff and wanted to take me on. In the end, one door closed and another open opened. I left Metro one day and came into Century the next. The job at Century was also a step up – they made me head of sport, offered me more money than I was on and told me I'd be working alongside Bobby Moncur, the former Newcastle United captain and the last man to lift a major trophy for the club – the Fairs Cup in 1969.

Bob and I did the commentary for two seasons on Century Radio and it was an amazing experience. He had such an influence on me professionally, and as a person. When I first met Bob, I had this rock-y, skater-boy sort of edge, walking in with my ripped jeans. Bob, with his shirt and tie on, took one look at me and said, 'Nope. You can't be wearing that.' I could tell he was thinking, *Who is this kid they've stuck me with?!* So Bob went about trying to make me treat commentary much more professionally, and I smartened up my act. If I ever turned up late, he'd give me a bollocking, in a friendly way, but in a manner that made sure I'd never do it again. He drove to all the games we commentated at, home and away, and he'd pick me up on the way. And as you can imagine, with Newcastle being so far north, that involved a lot of long motorway drives down south. He always used to tell me that if I wasn't there when he turned up outside my door, he'd go without me and find someone at the game who'd step up and do the commentary. Thankfully, we didn't ever have to put that threat to the test because I was always outside waiting for him, even if I was nursing the occa-sional Friday night hangover. 'Were you drinking last night, Pete?' 'No, no, who me?' I'd say, and as we sped away, he'd say, 'I can smell it on you, Pete!' I respected and admired Bob a lot and we'd talk about football for the whole journey, pretty much. The journeys flew by. Bob's a legend at St James' Park. He and his wife Camille go to every game. There's even a Bob Moncur Suite there and I always pop in and say hello and join them for a beer or a glass of wine. He's an amazing bloke and an inspiration, still commentating while he was going through chemotherapy. He never missed a single game.

I remember, soon after I'd joined Century in 2007, Bob and I were commentating on a game at St James' Park. One of our players missed a sitter early in the first half and I banged the desk in front of us in frustration. But the machine sitting on the desk that broadcasted the commentary over the airwaves suddenly died. I was frantically pressing all the buttons but there was nothing doing. Bob's asking me what's going on, but there doesn't seem to be any way to fix it. Then my phone starts ringing – it's the producer at Century telling me all he can hear is dead air and asking me what the hell's going on – and I'm saying, 'I don't know.' But then he can hear Bob's voice in the background saying, 'He punched the bloody desk and the machine's broken!' In the end, I put my mobile to my ear and broadcasted live to the radio station, while Bob, bless him, drove back to the studio to pick up another broadcasting machine. Luckily it was a home match, so it wasn't too far, through town and across the Tyne Bridge. I'm not sure which one of us drew the short straw, to be honest. Bob finally appears 20 minutes or so later towards the end of the half, sweating, with a face of thunder, carrying a new broadcasting machine under his arm. He hands it to me without a word and I'm scrambling under the desk to plug it in. And it's then that I realise that the other machine wasn't broken. The plug had just slipped out a bit, enough to turn it off. So I pushed the plug back in and everything came back to life.

Meanwhile, after Glenn Roeder left in May 2007, Sam Allardyce was soon announced as the new manager, an appointment that fans were sceptical about from day one. There was a perception that Big Sam's style of football wouldn't go down well on Tyneside, and this would prove to be the case. However, some huge news was coming from behind the scenes that was about to change everything. Sir John Hall had been looking to sell his majority stake in the club for a few years. And then, in late May 2006, he got a call from an agent asking if he'd sell his shares and inviting him down to a meeting in London to meet with an interested party. Hall travelled south and met billionaire CEO of Sports Direct, Mike Ashley, who'd just made over £900 million from floating Sports Direct on the stock market earlier in the year. Hall was surprised to find Ashley in a lawyer's office full of people, intent on striking out a deal there and then. Ashley wasn't interested in due diligence – the process that you normally undertake before a business deal to investigate the legal, fiscal and financial circumstances of the individual you're intending to do business with. Hall recalls imagining it was going to be a fairly short meeting and not even packing an overnight bag, but it took three days, and at the end of it he'd sold his family's 41.6 per cent stake in the club to Ashley for £55 million. Everyone was shocked by the decision. Freddy Shepherd and Sam Allardyce had no idea what was going on and Hall recalls getting 'slated' by his own son, Douglas, and Freddy Shepherd when they found out.

And as per UK takeover law, when someone acquires 30 per cent or more of a company, they are obliged to offer to buy the remaining shares at either the same price as the stake they've already bought or higher. Shepherd accepted Ashley's 101 pence per share offer for his 29.8 per cent stake in the club and other shareholders followed suit. By 15 June, he'd amassed over 75 per cent of the club's shares, triggering a full takeover.

In Hall's meeting with Ashley, Hall asked him why a businessman from down south was interested in a football club in the North East, and according to Hall, he said, 'Newcastle United is a brand, and we want to sell our products in the Far East. We think the two go together. Newcastle United will help us sell our goods in the Far East.' Maybe that struck a chord with fellow businessman Hall, I don't know. Hall admitted to feeling out of his depth when Roman Abramovich took over as owner of Chelsea, suddenly being able to pour hundreds of millions into his club, and he felt Ashley would do the same for Newcastle United. It was the era of the billionaire, not the local millionaire.

And so begins the darkest chapter in the Newcastle United story. The Mike Ashley era.

CHAPTER 5

THE **MIKE ASHLEY** ERA

To be honest, I wasn't sure whether to even talk about this era because I wanted this to be a book of positivity. But in order to underline the significance of what's happening at Newcastle United now, under Eddie Howe, you have to look back at what was, to put it mildly, an extremely difficult time under Mike Ashley's ownership. Also, it felt like ignoring a 15-year period would just look like I'm trying to pretend it didn't happen. And no one's going to learn anything from that. I feel like it needs to be talked about, so we can understand what went wrong and so we can hopefully never find ourselves in that position again.

Mike Ashley was greeted with support when he took over Newcastle United. He was a very wealthy British businessman. I was working in local radio when the news broke and I remember researching his net worth and thinking, *Wow – this guy's a big deal and this has got huge potential for the success of the club.* And I think Ashley came into the club wanting this to be a really success-ful venture. There was excitement when he was seen wearing a Newcastle United shirt in the director's box. He wasn't anything like other wealthy businessmen that took over football clubs. He was young, buying rounds in town, flashing the cash in night-clubs, talking about reducing the club's debt and even going to an away game in a white Transit van with supporters. There was an element of intrigue about him. The feeling that he's super wealthy but one of the guys. This would very quickly turn sour.

Sam Allardyce, who had been the appointment of former chairman Sir John Hall, only lasted for 24 games, and he left by 'mutual consent' on 9 January 2008 after eight months. His replacement was a massive, sensational surprise, especially as the man in question had retired from football in 2005. Nearly 11 years to the day since he resigned, club legend Kevin Keegan was being unveiled as our new manager. It was such a huge boost to the fans and the kind of move that indicated Ashley valued the history, heritage and supporters of our club. Ashley was suddenly a hero, and milked it for all it was worth, wearing a replica home shirt with 'King Kev No 1' on the back. He was quite the showman.

It was surreal at first to see Keegan in the dugout again, but the buzz was back at St James' Park. I remember there was a queue at the ticket office for season tickets the night it was announced. Newcastle United had a new ambitious owner and the best man possible back in the dugout – what could possibly go wrong? Unfortunately, Keegan must have realised pretty quickly that the club had declined massively since he left in 1997. The buzz faded within months, mainly because we went nine games without a win including batterings by Aston Villa, Man United and Liverpool. In a rare bit of good news during that time, Bobby Robson turned 75 on 18 February 2008 and the club had kept quiet about having a small 'head and shoulders' bust of Bobby made outside the players' entrance to the Milburn Stand. The plan was to unveil it when Bobby walked up to the game against Manchester United the following Saturday, joined by Kevin Keegan and visiting manager Alex Ferguson. The whole thing was kept a secret – not even Bobby's family knew. Bobby only saw it when he was walking up to the game, and he was completely overwhelmed, telling the crowd there: 'I'm a little lost for words as I had no idea this was going to happen … I am so proud and I am so thrilled at this. To be recognised like this is so pleasing. I would just like to thank everyone involved with doing this.'

I loved Bobby. I remember around that time my wife and I were lucky enough to have dinner with him and his wonderful wife Lady Elsie at his magnificent home in Durham. It was a night neither Steph nor I will ever forget. Funnily enough, around that same time Sky Sports had offered me the job as a presenter and Bobby really pushed me to take it, telling me it was a once in a lifetime opportunity. The subject of Steph being reluctant to move to London came up and Bobby said to her: 'Elsie didn't want to move to Eindhoven at first, she didn't want to move to Porto, or Barcelona, but everywhere we went, she loved it! Steph – move to London, you'll love it there!' And off the back of that chat, Steph moved down to London. I felt a real affinity with Bobby, along with so many others who had similar stories to mine. He was so welcoming, so kind, so encouraging. He was like a father to everyone.

On the pitch, things started coming together for Keegan, as well. In March and April 2008, there were convincing wins away at Spurs, and at home to Fulham, Reading and Sunderland. New club captain Michael Owen was firing on all cylinders, scoring seven times in the final nine games of the season, meaning we finished in 12th place. There was a sense that things might be looking up. Kevin Keegan was back, after all, and he'd steered us as close to success as it was possible to. But a wise man once said to me, 'If the wrong person owns the club, there's nobody inside it that can rescue it.' And that's exactly what sums up the Ashley era. Not even Keegan could rescue us.

The summer transfer window looked fairly promising, with Argentinian international Jonás Gutiérrez joining the club in July 2008 followed by countryman Fabricio Coloccini a few weeks later. They both went straight into the side to face Man United at Old Trafford on the first day of the season and both looked like the real deal in a solid 1–1 draw, which was a big improvement after the 11–1 hammering we'd taken on aggregate of the two games the previous season. But everything was far from solid behind the scenes. Disagreements over transfer policy between Keegan and Ashley had spilled out into the open and there was the sense that this wasn't going to resolve itself. Keegan resigned on 4 September 2008 and issued a statement via the League Managers Association that reiterated something that most fans were already aware of:

'I've been working desperately hard to find a way forward with the directors, but sadly that has not proved possible.

It's my opinion that a manager must have the right to manage and that clubs should not impose upon any manager any player that he does not want. It remains my fervent wish to see Newcastle United do well in the future and I feel incredibly sorry for the players, staff and most importantly the supporters. I have been left with no choice other than to leave.'

Keegan talks about what led him to that point in his book *My Life in Football*. It seemed to reach a head after Keegan recalls being told by Tony Jimenez, who'd been hired as vice president (player recruitment) shortly after Keegan was appointed on 16 January 2008, that they would be buying 22-year-old Spanish striker Xisco from Deportivo for £5.7 million and acquiring 26-year-old Ignacio González from Valencia (in a deal that involved Valencia buying the player and then loaning him out to Newcastle United 24 hours later). These were two players that nobody at Newcastle United had ever seen play and it turned out that the whole thing had been a favour to two agents from South America, who had helped Newcastle United land Fabricio Coloccini and Jonás Gutiérrez. According to Kevin, after expressing serious doubts about González to director of football Dennis Wise (who had been appointed to the position on 29 January 2008), Wise told Keegan that they could just 'park' González at the academy. Keegan phoned Mike Ashley, who didn't seem to be familiar with the González loan but offered to pay for it himself rather than out of the club's transfer budget if it would make Keegan happier. Keegan didn't like the look of it at all and that's what triggered his resignation. Looking back on what happened in his second spell at the club, Keegan said: 'I came up against a wall of incompetence, deceit and arrogance – you couldn't make up some of the things that happened at Newcastle under this regime. It was a tragicomedy.'

Soon after Keegan left, Alan Shearer was fired as ambassador for the club after criticising Keegan's exit, the club's transfer policy and for calling the set-up of the club 'strange'. Two club legends gone. The fans had had enough and weren't afraid to tell Ashley. They absolutely hated him and it seemed for a second that he finally got it, issuing the statement:

'I have the interests of Newcastle United at heart. I have listened to you. You want me out. That is what I am now trying to do but it won't happen overnight and it may not happen at all if a buyer does not come in. You don't need to demonstrate against me again because I have got the message. Any further action will only have an adverse effect on the team. As fans of Newcastle United you need to spend your energy getting behind, not me, but the players who need your support.'

Looking back at that period of Keegan's second spell in charge at the club under Ashley's ownership, it felt like Keegan was appointed, under false pretences, as a figurehead to placate the fans. Fans felt misled, confused and cheated by this, and Dennis Wise became the focal point for the anger. The details about the breakdown of Keegan's relationship with Ashley, Wise and Jimenez came out in court in 2009 after Keegan sued for constructive dismissal – a case that Keegan won. It didn't help Wise (or the club's case) that on 31 January 2008 he gave an interview from the chairman's office at the club, published on the club's website the next day and in the national press, in which he said: 'He [Kevin] has the final word [on transfers] and then no one else. I'm not going to do things like bring players in behind his back. I'm not into that and everything that happens will be run past him and he'll say yes, as I say, or he'll say no.' That was completely at odds with the club's position in the tribunal for Keegan's constructive dismissal in October 2009, in which it argued that it was 'implicit from the discussions [on 16 January 2008 which resulted in Keegan being appointed the manager of the club], in particular from the structure of the club as it was explained to Mr Keegan ... that he would not have the final say.' The 'structure' they were talking about is the so-called continental model where a director of football and vice-president traditionally have the final say on transfers.

It came down to the fact that Ashley didn't give Keegan all the tools that he needed to do his job – the final say on signings. That power lay with Dennis Wise and Tony Jimenez. If Ashley had instead relied on Keegan to control signings, something he proved he could do fantastically well during his first spell at the club, we might have been facing a different future. But Ashley made a series of really bad calls, which made both the supporters and the club itself suffer. At Newcastle United, you have to harness the potential of the fans and you have to have the whole city pulling in the same direction. If you are not going to be honest with them, you're disrespecting the people that are putting their hard-earned cash in your pocket.

The Newcastle United fans' feelings towards Dennis Wise remain incredibly bitter even now. One of the toughest weeks of my life came after I was photographed at an 'England Legends' event in 2019 alongside Wise. Looking back it was naïve and idiotic of me to post the picture, but I took my eye off the ball with regards to social media and a large number of fans made their feelings known. I quickly deleted the picture but the damage was done. The reality was that I was hosting a screening of England v The Netherlands in central London and the two main guests were Paul Ince and Dennis Wise. It was dubbed as a 'Legends Dinner' and largely populated by Chelsea fans, so Wise, their former captain, was warmly applauded into the room. I didn't think anything at the time when the professional photographer gathered the three of us for a photo, but after I posted it on Twitter, I was suddenly getting thousands of mentions. Somebody told me I wasn't welcome at St James' Park again. Anyone who says abuse on social media doesn't bother them is lying. I was sick with stress for weeks. All over a photo.

The weird thing about working in sports broadcasting is that you are regularly working alongside people that are villains at various clubs. There are numerous opposition players and ex-managers that Newcastle United fans despise and if I'm honest I've probably worked with most of them at one point or another. After this Dennis Wise debacle I posted a short statement explaining what had happened and then as per usual Keegan himself saved the day. I was at an event with him and former Sunderland manager Peter Reid a few weeks later and I explained the story. They laughed and said, 'Come on then, let's put this thing to bed for you,' and we posed for a picture of them with their thumbs down and getting me in a headlock. Order had been restored.

• • •

Chris Hughton took over as caretaker manager after Keegan's resignation. Hughton had been our first-team coach since February 2008, but after going three games without a win, Joe Kinnear was hired as 'interim' manager. In late November, Mike Ashley gave him the job permanently, but Kinnear fell ill on 7 February 2009 just before a game against West Bromwich Albion and it was later announced that he would need a triple heart bypass operation. Hughton (along with Colin Calderwood and Paul Barron) took over for the next few games, but despite a win away at West Brom, they went through a bad spell of defeats. Relegation loomed large and time was running out.

Ashley sought a saviour. So he turned to Alan Shearer. It was, which has been a common theme in this book, a gamble, but this time it was an instantly popular one. Shearer had no managerial experience, but there was no way that he was going to turn down the chance to save his club from relegation. We had eight games left of the season, were in 18th place and two points adrift of safety. It was a perilous position. Here's what Alan Shearer had to say about it to me:

'It was always my intention to go back into the game. And when the Newcastle offer came along, I didn't really have a choice because my club was on its knees and about to appoint their fourth manager that season. I couldn't wait – Newcastle were about to be relegated. They had to try something different and I was that something different.'

Despite the tide of optimism after Alan's appointment, we weren't able to convert that encouragement into points, going down 2–0 to Chelsea at St James' Park. The noise difference before the game and after were poles apart. It was silent at the final whistle. Relegation was supposed to be unthinkable for a club as big as ours, but every single Geordie in that stadium was thinking about it. We were all hoping for the fabled shot in the arm a team gets from a new managerial appointment – especially a club legend like Shearer. Andy Carroll rescued a draw in the next game at the Britannia against Stoke but we were lucky to get away with that. A tricky away game against Spurs proved beyond us, but the home game against Portsmouth at St James' was a must-win. A six-pointer.

We'd only scored four times in the past eight matches so Shearer went for a front three: Owen, Martins and Mark Viduka. To be fair, we managed 14 shots and four on target, but it just wasn't happening and Pompey nearly won it with a header that hit the post in the 82nd minute. It ended 0–0 and it was starting to look like we were down. Next up was Liverpool at Anfield – not the ideal match given that they were chasing a league title and had won six of the last seven games, the only 'blip' being a 4–4 draw against Arsenal. We got battered 3–0, Joey Barton losing his head with a two-footed challenge on Xabi Alonso, who was keeping possession by the corner late on in the game. I remember all the Liverpool fans pointing at Shearer in the dugout and chanting, 'Stayed on the telly – you should have stayed on the telly!' Despite the dire situation, it was fairly good crack from them. Up in the commentary box I didn't know whether to laugh or cry.

But then came the ray of hope. A home game against Boro. Tragically, a Habib Beye own goal only three minutes in was the nightmare start everyone dreaded. Steven Taylor powered home a header just six minutes later and some of the anxiety ebbed away, but a draw wasn't going to be good enough. Shearer took a chance with 20 minutes left, the scores still 1–1, taking Owen off for Martins. But it turned out to be a genius move because within about five seconds, Martins slotted the ball past Brad Jones after a wayward pass. Boro very nearly equalised about a minute later and a very tense 15 minutes followed before Peter Løvenkrands answered our prayers four minutes from time and made it 3–1. The relief around the stadium was huge. It was our first win in 11 games. And more importantly, we were out of the bottom three. I remember for the first time in months thinking, *We might actually be OK. This will be the catalyst.* Even Shearer was bouncing afterwards when he came down to do the interviews. It felt like a massive corner had been turned. There were two games left, next up was Fulham at home and then a trip to Aston Villa. We were almost there.

Here's what Alan told me about that period:

'Sometimes you get a kick [when a new manager starts] and I was so confident after beating Middlesbrough at home, and as it turned out we just needed another point after that, but it wasn't meant to be. I think when you've had four managers in one season, I just think it doesn't take much common sense to work out that there's huge issues within that football club. Three managers before me went in and tried to sort things out but couldn't, both on the pitch and off the pitch. It was a tough one to go into to begin with for me but I loved it. I really enjoyed the test and the pressure you're put under and everything else and that's why I thought I was going to stay. And I was determined of that. I was going to stay and bring the club back up. But no regrets, I made the right decision at the right time – it just wasn't meant to be.'

The high of the Middlesbrough win disintegrated five days later when we lost 1–0 at home to Fulham. And we travelled to Aston Villa on the final day of the season on 24 March 2009 needing something, but it never came. A deflected own goal from Damien Duff (who was now playing as a makeshift left-back) capped off a disastrous season from start to finish. It was the end of 16 straight seasons in the Premier League and the end of my time as a radio commentator. I'd been trying to continue as a commentator whilst working at Sky Sports and it had all become too much. As the final whistle blew I made the decision to pass the commentary mantle to someone else and focus on Sky Sports. I remember feeling really down and emotional, much like all the fans either at the stadium or listening from home. The Aston Villa fans showed no sympathy and held up a massive banner saying 'Sob on the Tyne'. When I walked back into the press room, Sky Sports News was live on all the screens and the Hull City manager Phil Brown was singing into a microphone to all the Hull fans, having just survived relegation at our expense despite a 1–0 defeat to Manchester United. I felt sick when I saw it. Bob and I barely spoke a word on the drive home. It was the last time we worked together on the radio.

Shearer told reporters that 'The three worst teams deserved to go down. Unfortunately Newcastle were one of them. You get what you deserve after 38 games. I'm hurt, I'm raw inside, as are a lot of people in the dressing room. Big changes need to be made.'

Even Alan Shearer wasn't able to save us. It was a bleak day. The future looked very uncertain. The club was in total disarray.

And this was all happening at a period of great uncertainty for me professionally. While I'd landed a dream job at Sky Sports as a presenter in February 2009, months had gone by and I was still logging tapes and recording the odd voiceover segment. I'd made the mistake of telling everyone I knew that I'd got the presenter job at Sky Sports, so, of course, they expected to see me on telly as soon as I started. I kept getting texts like: 'Are you sure you're a presenter, mate?!'

Then, suddenly, I got my shot. I was petrified beforehand and to be honest it showed. My presenting must have been absolutely terrible that first night. I've never had the desire to watch it back. What I knew was that I was way out of my depth. I wasn't used to the Sky office environment, where it's all glass and there are TV screens everywhere, so when I heard the countdown in my earpiece reach 'one' to signify that I'm live, my face is suddenly all around the whole building. It's like you're on *The Truman Show* or something. It hit me how many people were watching and that I was live on national TV. Way too many things were going around my head while I was trying to read an autocue. And before I'd finished my segment, I knew that I wasn't good enough to be there. I just wasn't ready. The whole situation felt like I'd been playing for a small football team and I was one of the best players there, scoring loads of goals, and then suddenly a Premier

League club signs me and I spend weeks on the bench, before finally getting my shot and then fluffing it. I thought to myself, *You are the worst player here by a mile.* And it wasn't just me that knew it. Everyone did.

At ITV Tyne Tees, where I'd landed my first presenting gig in 2008, I'd have the entire day to prepare for a simple two-minute bulletin in the evening. There were plenty of rehearsals and everything was very relaxed. But now at Sky, I was not only presenting an entire four-hour show: I was also dealing with my producer talking into my earpiece to update the cricket, golf or rugby league, then there was breaking news that someone had broken their leg or moved clubs. It was mayhem in my ear and it was so hard to concentrate on everything at once. I worked out that I'd probably done more screen time in that first presenting shift at Sky Sports News than I had in an entire year at Tyne Tees TV. It all just felt like too much too soon. I wasn't just dealing with Newcastle United any more, I wasn't even just dealing with football – I was dealing with every sports team in the country and beyond!

The thing is: you can't really train for the experience of being a presenter. You just have to see if you can deal with everything coming at you at a million miles an hour. It was sink or swim. I didn't feel like I swam, though. I felt like I clung on to a branch for long enough to avoid drowning. It was a real knock to my confidence. I reacted by trying to up my game, imitating the style of other presenters, coming into work really early, taking time to mentally prepare myself, but it didn't seem as though anything was going to make me better at it. Six months later, I told myself that this really wasn't working and that I needed to leave. My wife, Steph, wasn't settling – I was spending half the week down in West London and the other half of the week up in Newcastle – and I just wanted to go back home and to the life I had before on local TV and local radio. I felt beaten by the experience at Sky Sports. My dream felt like it was over.

The weird thing is, that difficult period for me at work actually ended up becoming a huge turning point. I accepted that I wasn't good enough to work there and it made me relax. I stopped putting myself under as much pressure, got through one presenting shift at a time and told myself to just make it through to the end of the year. And then on my way out of the building about a month later, my boss stopped me in the corridor and told me I'd really improved in the last few weeks. It massively surprised me and it was the first compliment I'd had while working at Sky. But, I suppose after doing a few three- to four-hour shifts a week, my experience was racking up quickly. I tried to keep it light-hearted and accept that I might have a bad shift once in a while, though I knew that I'd done enough good ones for it to not knock my confidence. And if I did make mistakes, I'd try to make a joke out of them.

Meanwhile, Mike Ashley was making mistakes but us fans weren't laughing. He made a lot of noise about trying to find a buyer for the club, but nothing came of that – something that became a recurring theme. No new players came in, but some big ones left: Owen, Viduka and Løvenkrands were out of contract and Martins, Duff, Beye and [Sébastien] Bassong were all sold.

Hughton was back in temporary charge. Shearer's future at the club was still up in the air. In his interview to celebrate Kevin Keegan's 70th birthday with The Athletic in 2021, he revealed what happened: 'That summer, having presented my plans to secure promotion at the first time of asking, I waited for Mike Ashley to call me back. I'm still waiting.'

• • •

Football and everything else in the world paused when we heard some desperately sad news. On 31 July 2009, our Black and White Knight, Sir Bobby Robson, had died peacefully at home.

For a while, everyone forgot about the terrible situation the club was in. We were united in grief over the passing of a legend. A gentleman and one of the finest people I've ever known.

José Mourinho, who had famously been Bobby's translator at Sporting Lisbon in 1992 and had followed him as his assistant at Porto and Barcelona, becoming a long-time friend, said: 'It is difficult to accept such a person is no longer with us. But he is immortal because he leaves in everybody who knows him a mark of his personality – a great coach but, more than that, a great person.' Alex Ferguson said: 'I mourn the passing of a great friend, a wonderful individual, a tremendous football man and somebody with passion and knowledge of the game that was unsurpassed.' On *ITV News*, Paul Gascoigne said: 'I'm speechless. I'm devastated. Bobby was like my second dad … I can't describe how much he meant to me. I've just been crying for three hours, and I've come to see my mum and my dad. It's just unbelievable.'

Tributes came in from players, managers, coaching staff, politicians, members of the royal family and people across the world. He touched so many people. He was the grandfather of football. I felt so privileged that he knew who I was and that I'd got to spend time with him. He was also a great help to me as a young journalist. My first season was his last season at Newcastle and in that short period of time he taught me a lot. The radio documentary tribute I made about him was one of the things I'm most proud of in my life. After he retired, he'd listen to my commentaries on the radio and come up to me and make comments about something I'd said. That was absolutely mind-boggling to me, that Sir Bobby was interested in what I had to say.

He was truly a great man.

. . .

The 2009–10 season began with Chris Hughton back as caretaker manager. Attendance at the first home game was way down, at just under 37,000, but a hat-trick from Shola Ameobi lifted the place. I watched that match in a pub in London. It was really odd because it was the first match in years that I hadn't been there doing the commentary. I'd love to say it was difficult to be away, but in truth I remember having a brilliant afternoon. I was drinking pints in a beer garden, the match was on the big screen and there were loads of London-based Geordies in there all singing. I'd missed watching the matches as a fan and it was good to have the opportunity to do that again. My mum and dad of course were both there in our season tickets and I remember my dad talking about the number of empty seats in their section. Despite that we never even considered getting rid of our season tickets as many others did around that time. It's a decision that has paid off massively now, but I totally understand anyone who decided to walk away.

We won five of our first six games and were top of the table. After winning back-to-back Manager of the Month awards in August and September 2009, Hughton was offered the job permanently. It began to look as though we might not be hanging around in the Championship for too long, although Mike Ashley did his best to derail the improved mood with another PR disaster, this time announcing that he intended to sell off the naming rights to St James' Park. I'm not sure you could have made a more tone-deaf move, to be honest.

By Christmas, though, with eight wins out of the last nine games, we were flying. We only lost one more game in the whole season, were automatically promoted by Easter and won the title with two games to spare, amassing 102 points. The feel-good factor was back. I'd started to cover a few of the away games as a Sky Sports reporter and I was at Plymouth the night we sealed promotion with a 2–0 away win. I remember interviewing the likes of Kevin Nolan, Joey Barton and Andy Carroll in the tunnel afterwards and thinking, *How the hell did this lot end up in the Championship?!* But the job was done and we were heading back to the big time.

Then the next season, 2010–11, started inconsistently, losing on the opening day 3–0 at Man United, followed by a huge 6–0 win against Aston Villa at St James' Park with Andy Carroll completing his hat-trick in second-half injury time. Three wins on the trot in October and early November, including a very pleasing 5–1 thrashing of Sunderland and an away win at Arsenal (our first at Arsenal in 10 years), gave the fans something to cheer about. But we went five games without a win over November/December. Yeah, I accept that's a fairly bad run, but not a catastrophic one, especially given that we'd won the previous three. We were 11th in the table. And yet Hughton was sacked. It was another bewildering decision.

At the time of writing, Chris Hughton still has the highest win percentage of any manager in Newcastle United's history.* To us fans, who'd really warmed to the guy, we were left scratching our heads. There were rumours that Chris had lost the dressing room, but that didn't chime with what captain Kevin Nolan said to *The Sun* soon afterwards: 'We are all upset that Chris is going. He helped a lot of the lads here with their careers when he was a coach and then as manager.' Defender Sol Campbell echoed what a lot of us were thinking, putting it simply: 'It makes no sense.' José Enrique, our player of the season the previous year, was more direct: 'If they're going to fire someone as good as Chris, they have to then bring in a big name, someone who has won trophies.'

It was another strange decision under the Ashley ownership that annoyed and frustrated players, fans, former players, fellow managers and members of the media. It was almost like Ashley was his own worst enemy. As soon as something good was happening,

* While he was in charge from 1 June 2009 to 6 December 2010, if we don't count John Carver, who had a 100 per cent record after winning the only match he was in charge for.

it felt like he wanted to sabotage it. After Chris brought us straight up from the Championship, we weren't expecting to be competing for Champions League places. A respectable mid-table finish after coming up is what we were after really.

Alan Pardew was hired three days later. It went down terribly with the fans when it was announced. It was another random name from the wilderness. It felt like Joe Kinnear mark two. Technically, he was the eighth manager since Ashley took over ownership of the club in 2007. Hundreds of fans protested at Pardew's first game in charge at St James' Park, voicing their appreciation for Hughton and their anger at Ashley. But the team made a solid start under Pardew, beating Liverpool 3–1 at St James' Park and we thought, *Maybe, just maybe, things might work out OK.*

That first season back in the Premier League was full of brief highs, like the incredible comeback against Arsenal, levelling the score at 4–4 after trailing 0–4 at half-time, and longer lows, like the FA Cup third round loss to League Two Stevenage. But, to be fair, some credit must go to Pardew. The following season, we had a blinder of a season, finishing fifth in the league, above Chelsea and Liverpool and qualifying for the Europa League play-offs. Graham Carr had been doing some fantastic work that season as chief scout (he'd joined in 2010), helping to sign Yohan Cabaye (June 2011) and Demba Ba (June 2011) as well as Cheick Tioté (August 2010) and Hatem Ben Arfa (January 2011 after his season-long loan) the previous season.

For a short time, it felt like things were going the right way. Pardew even won the LMA Manager of the Year Award and the

Premier League Manager of the Season for 2011–12 along the way (the only Newcastle United manager to win both awards), but the club didn't react to finishing fifth by thinking big and trying to capitalise on their success. Instead, our top scorer, Demba Ba, was sold to Chelsea for £7 million in January 2013. We'd only had him for 18 months and he'd come in for nothing. Yohan Cabaye went the following year for around £19 million to Paris Saint-Germain. We'd bought him for £4 million. It was clear what was happening. The club wanted to turn around players they'd bought cheaply or for nothing and make money, but it felt like nobody was ever being honest with the fans. And we were losing other players to smaller Premier League clubs because they were willing to pay a bit more on the wage front than we were. Newcastle United fans could just about understand losing players to big clubs but losing players to clubs at the bottom end of the Premier League was hard to take. It would have been easier to swallow if someone had told us the truth.

And while we fans were getting angered by these sorts of decisions, Pardew never seemed to show any frustration about it. I work with Pardew on occasion now and he's a decent bloke, but he didn't reflect the disgruntlement of the fans, and that kept them apart from him. His continued defence of Ashley meant that the success we enjoyed in that brief period always felt a bit tainted. I understand why he did it – trashing the owner tends to lead to being handed your P45 – but we got the impression that he and Ashley were on the same page. And anyone with a good working relationship with Ashley was never going to be popular with the fans. Pardew was caught between a rock and a hard place, really.

Then there were the completely unheard of eight-year contracts that Ashley handed out to Pardew and his coaching staff in 2012, something that goalkeeping coach Andy Woodman explained was first talked about when Ashley spotted him after midnight in a bar-restaurant in Jesmond. Woodman assumed he was in trouble when Ashley started walking over to him, seeing it was late on a Friday night before a game the next day. But according to Woodman, Ashley wasn't unhappy at all – he started buying shots for everyone before he told Woodman: 'You've done a great job – I'm going to give you an eight-year contract tomorrow.' The next day, after talking to Pardew about it, Woodman went to Mike Ashley to turn the offer down because it was longer than Pardew's, Steve Stone's (the first team coach) and John Carver's (the assistant manager) and so would have caused all sorts of internal problems. In the end, Ashley offered them all eight-year contracts. It was all quite strange, but not out of keeping from a man who was notoriously cavalier in his business dealings.

John Carver took over at the end of 2014 as temporary head coach until the end of the season. We went on a terrible run from 4 March to 2 May, losing eight games in a row, but a draw and a win in the final three games was enough for us to survive another season. Carver and Stone were both let go in June and Steve McLaren was appointed head coach. He was also, strangely, appointed to the club's board of directors (Ashley had stepped down as a director), and even more strangely, had practically no contact from Ashley. McLaren admitted in an interview with Chronicle Live that: 'I just wanted the job and didn't find out the real vision, direction, what success looked like … and how I was to communicate with the owner, who's the most important person at a football club. Usually, you communicate not in pairs but in threes, so it's always, say, myself, the CEO and the owner, or myself, the technical director/sporting director and the owner. I never had that and that was a massive thing that I didn't really know the vision.'

He went on to explain that in his first press conference, only two members of the press were allowed to interview him, with 26 excluded. That set him off 'on a downer already and I couldn't be honest with my messages to the press'. Again, honesty was missing, the key characteristic that Kevin Keegan would later pinpoint when Eddie Howe called him up after taking the job in 2021 to ask for his advice.

McLaren only won seven games during his tenure and was sacked in March 2016. He talked about finding out weeks into the job that all the staff at the club were made to pay for tickets to watch games at St James' Park, so none of them went. And that meant none of them saw 'the fruition of that work on a Saturday'. McLaren felt that it all fed into the sense, as he told Chronicle Live, that 'the culture and environment wasn't conducive to real success'.

• • •

Rafa Benítez's appointment was a nice surprise to the fans. It felt like we'd hired a winner – the guy had won La Liga and the UEFA Cup with unfancied Valencia, the Champions League in 2005 and the FA Cup in 2006 with Liverpool, the Europa League with Chelsea in 2013, the Coppa Italia with Napoli in 2014, and he'd been named UEFA Manager of the Year twice. And not only was he a winner – he'd had experience of leading big clubs back to where they should be. Benítez was a stellar appointment for us at the time. And in the time he was at Newcastle United, he turned us into a club that the fans could believe in again, and that was no mean feat in the desperately bleak 15 years that Mike Ashley owned the club.

Rafa did himself a favour by calling Newcastle United 'a legendary club' in his first interview, adding 'C'mon, Toon Army!' You could see that he had passion, determination and respect for the club. But the club that he inherited was sitting in 19th place in the table, having won only six games in the first 28 of the season. Nine points away from safety, it looked pretty desperate. And then, after three defeats in four games, we were staring down the barrel. But then we conjured up a six-game unbeaten stretch at the end of the season. We drew with Man City and Liverpool, won against Swansea and Crystal Palace and battered Spurs in the final game of the season 5–1, but it still wasn't enough to save us, finishing the season on 37 points and, agonisingly, two adrift of Sunderland. We were down already but the fans wanted Rafa to stay. St James' was packed to the rafters. I think about a lot of other clubs in that situation, and the ground would be barely half-full. But there wasn't a seat free and everyone was singing 'Rafa Benítez – we want you to stay' and waving Rafa banners and flags from kick-off to after the final whistle. And during that game, we walloped Spurs, who were chasing a second-place finish in the table. For a team going down, there was no negativity around St

James' Park. And it was all the more extraordinary because Rafa had only been our manager for 10 games!

But it was what he did next that really catapulted the fans' love affair with Rafa. He stayed with us. Everyone expected him to leave the club. We couldn't imagine that a manager as big as Benítez would stay after the club went down to the Championship. But he did, and that loyalty, commitment and dedication goes a long way in the Toon.

Rafa brought us straight back up at the first time of asking, winning the Championship. And on our return to our rightful place in the Premier League, we finished 10th after a decent season. That's what you want after heading back to the big league. A solid, mid-table finish that you can build on. He didn't quite manage that in the next season, but we finished 13th, and for a club whose fans, and manager's ambitions aren't supported by the owner, that's about the best you can hope for. He never got any money to spend. And he publicly criticised Ashley for it, and while that won him a lot of respect from the fans, who felt like Rafa spoke for them, it probably didn't win him any friends in the boardroom.

In an open letter that he wrote to fans to explain what was going on, he mentioned that game against Spurs:

'What we have had here – your support, your affection and your passion – has been unbelievable for me. St James' Park has been always special, the 5-1 win against Tottenham, 15-05-2016, was so emotional that since that day I have always felt as though I belonged at Newcastle and I thank you for making me feel so welcome and at home … I wanted to stay, but I didn't just want to sign an extended contract, I wanted to be part of a project.

Unfortunately, it became increasingly clear to me that those at the top of the club did not share the same vision.'

All of the managers under the Ashley ownership were told that they had a very limited budget and I think they were trying their best to work within the parameters they'd been given. Rafa Benítez was the only one who tried to break down those barriers. He publicly spoke about the untapped potential of the club (which I'm sure went down like a sh*t sandwich with Ashley and co.) and the fans loved him for it, but he left because he got frustrated that his hands were tied. In August 2019, he wrote in The Athletic about his reasons for not accepting what the club offered him after Lee Charnley had claimed that Benítez's decision to leave was financially motivated.

'Newcastle's board had a year to sort out my contract but, when we met after the end of last season [2017–18], they didn't make me a proper offer. They told me they didn't want to invest in the academy or the training ground … After that meeting, I knew they would not come back with a serious offer and, when it arrived, 19 days later, it was for the same salary as three years earlier and with less control over signings. After three years of unfulfilled promises, I didn't trust them.'

What a lot of the managers who were brought in under Ashley's tenure did was to say publicly that we couldn't compete with the top clubs. *We can't do this, we can't do that.* It just didn't sit right with the fans. And while we were being fed this, we looked

THE MIKE ASHLEY ERA

around us at St James' Park and saw so many potential revenue streams not being taken advantage of. The advertising around the stadium was completely Sports Direct, but the club didn't receive any money for that for a long time. Why on earth did that happen rather than open it up to other companies, who would have paid for the premium advertising space. It felt like everything was done on the cheap and nothing was ever anywhere near its potential.

. . .

Going back to that first week of November 2009, when the club announced plans to sell the naming rights to St James' Park and received fierce condemnation in Newcastle and from the wider football community, managing director Derek Llambias, with his tail between his legs, appeared a few days later in front of the cameras to 'clarify' the club's position. 'We could have worded it better, and that's why we came out to explain what we're trying to achieve ... with the renaming it was always going to be whatever brand it was, @St James' Park.' It was clearly a backtracking PR panic and nobody bought it (in two senses). You'd think they would have avoided revisiting the subject, but, amazingly, they came back to it in November 2011 with the announcement that St James' Park would be renamed the Sports Direct Arena. Here was the statement from the club:

'Newcastle United have today announced plans to license the full naming rights to the club's stadium following consultation with international branding experts.

The board are committed to generating additional commercial revenue from advertising and sponsorship opportunities.

The original naming rights proposal, launched in November 2009, invited sponsors to link their brand to St. James' Park, but this did not prove commercially attractive.

As such, the club will now seek a sponsor who will be granted full naming rights. Until such time the stadium will be renamed the Sports Direct Arena.'

It was an utter disgrace. St James' Park has been the name of the ground since 1892. It is part of the fabric of the city and everyone who lives in it. St James' Park even predates the name of the football club – Newcastle United, which dates back to December 1892, after the directors of the club Newcastle East End (which had just become the dominant team in the city after their rival club, West End FC, ran into financial trouble and ended up being absorbed by Newcastle East End in May 1892) decided they'd go for a new club name to draw bigger crowds and reflect the whole city better, so they put it to a public vote. 'Newcastle United' emerged as the winning name and it seemed like a good decision, reflecting the combination of the two teams. St James' Park also predates Newcastle wearing our famous black-and-white stripes, which we did for the first time at the beginning of the 1894–95 season. Before that, the newly formed Newcastle United wore red shirts and white shorts! St James' Park is our heritage and history, and it should never have been up for discussion.

Wonga, the controversial payday loan company, or to use their terminology 'digital finance company', agreed a sponsorship deal with the club in October 2012. It also secured naming rights for the stadium (not that anyone had actually ever called it the Sports

Direct Arena; the council even refused to rename the signs to the stadium, with Labour councillor Henri Murison saying: 'As far as the fans and Newcastle City Council are concerned, the home of Newcastle United will always be known as St James' Park'). But, in an extremely rare bit of good news at that time, a spokesperson for Wonga announced that they were going to restore the ground's name. 'We listened over the last three days and we saw what really matters to the fans. Football is an emotional sport and it's obviously really important to them. We listened to what they wanted and that is why we have done it.' It's a sad state of affairs when it takes Wonga to do the right thing.

Unfortunately, that wasn't the end of the renaming saga. I remember turning up to a home game in May 2013 and finding the entire roof of the Gallowgate End, which is kind of sacred to supporters, had been painted with SportsDirect.com because Ashley wanted it visible to planes that flew over. The whole place was a giant advert so he could sell cheap sportswear. Almost all of the ground chanted, 'What the f*****g hell is that?', except for the fans in the Gallowgate End, because they couldn't actually see it and must have wondered what the hell was going on. It was incredible how much the negativity from the stands just translated onto the pitch. There'd be some games when we were 1–0 up, but rather than cheering the team on the chanting would quickly turn. The most popular chants were always anti-Ashley ones. They sang those more than any others. Home games almost felt like a hindrance to our players, such was the negativity floating around the ground.

I was writing my column in the matchday programme at the time and it was so difficult. Every week, I spent ages trying to dredge up some positivity, but that got thrown back in my hashtags with people posting #onthepayroll. For what it's worth I don't get paid for my column in the programme. I do it for the love of the football club.

Eventually, I got a phone call from the media team at the club telling me that they didn't want me to do my column any more but they never gave me the reasons behind it. I think I'd got to a point where, as a fan, I'd started not being able to contain my frustration and I'd written some stuff that the club took issue with. I remember saying in one column that after a transfer window where we didn't buy anyone, it felt like a missed opportunity. I wasn't expecting that part to get printed but it was. I just didn't care any more. The phone call followed soon after that. What was great was that as soon as the takeover happened in 2021, I got another call from the media office. 'Would you like to resume your column?' I was asked. It was a lovely gesture. *I was back!*

I even think that Mike Ashley wanted the club to be success-ful but just made some really bad decisions and never harnessed the potential of the football club, which is something that the combination of Kevin Keegan and Sir John Hall did brilliantly, as did Sir Bobby and Freddy Shepherd, and as are Eddie Howe and the new ownership.

The problem for any manager in that period, even when Rafa took over, was that there were always chants at the ground about Ashley. For almost the entirety of Ashley's ownership, I can't remember not hearing chants telling him to get out of our club. And that makes it very difficult for whoever is in the job. In that final Rafa season, Newcastle had a new front three – Miguel Almirón, Salomón Rondón and Ayoze Pérez – and they had an understanding and it was exciting. There'd be matches where I'd look at my dad and say, 'We're not bad, you know!' but as with the whole of Ashley's ownership, as soon as we were moving in the right direction on the pitch, something would change. Pérez left in July 2019 for £20 million and Rondón was never offered a deal to make his hugely impressive loan spell at the club permanent. When Rafa left in June 2019, a lot of people gave up their season tickets and walked away from the football club. They just couldn't stomach it any more. I completely understand that.

My mum and dad sat through it in the Milburn Stand and they're now so pleased they did keep their season tickets. I think they stuck with it because it was such a great opportunity to see me and the grandkids and experience the game that we all love together. It was always a time to have a beer, a pie, a chat and watch the match. It was less about the football on the field and the politics off it. It was more about family coming together some-where that we always had.

Ashley made some good moves. Commissioning a bust for Bobby's 75th birthday was a fitting gesture. Bringing back Keegan and hiring Shearer were hugely popular decisions with the supporters and I think they were done for the right reasons. But he didn't back these two legends of the club and give them a chance. He let them fail by not giving them the respect they deserved.

And that was a massive no-no for Newcastle Untied fans. There was just no way back for Ashley after all that, whatever he did.

Mike Ashley gave his first ever interview in May 2015 on Sky Sports just before the final game of the season, against West Ham, a game we had to win. He admitted that responsibility for the situation they found themselves in lay at 'my door' and talked about his ambition to win a trophy or secure a top-four finish. For a second, it felt like *Great! Here we go then!* but nothing ended up happening because we managed to beat West Ham and avoid relegation, so he didn't feel like he needed to. And to make matters worse, the way the club treated Jonás Gutiérrez, a player the fans absolutely loved, was terrible. He'd revealed that he had testicular cancer in September 2014 and was undergoing a final session of chemotherapy. After battling through that, he came on as a sub at St James' against Man United in March 2015 to a fantastic reception from the fans. At Anfield, when he came on as a sub, the whole stadium rose to their feet to applaud him. In that all-or-nothing game against West Ham, Gutiérrez produced a man of the match performance, setting one goal up and scoring from outside the box in the 85th minute in front of the Gallowgate to secure our Premier League status. 'Can there be a more popular goalscorer? The man who knows the true meaning of survival,' commentator Peter Drury said as St James' erupted. 'I'm really proud to be a Geordie,' Gutiérrez said in his post-match interview. An absolute hero. But a week later, he was released from his contract by the club.

It was a ridiculous story that I remember breaking live one night on Sky Sports News. Club hero Ryan Taylor, who had immortalised himself for his 'over the wall' free kick against Sunderland in 2011 but whose career had been plagued by injury, had got a phone call (him and Jonás were both together doing their coaching badges at the time, because they were heading towards the end of their careers and that's something quite a few senior players do) to tell him he wasn't going to have his contract renewed. Ryan was asked if Jonás was with him, so he passed his phone over to Jonás who was given the same news. They didn't even make two separate phone calls. They chose to kill two magpies with one stone. Both players were popular figures with the supporters and they deserved more than to be ditched in one bloody phone call. You simply couldn't imagine things like that happening under Sir Bobby, Keegan or under Eddie Howe today. The guys deserved a proper send-off and a chance to say good-bye. But the way they were dumped was ruthless and lacked any emotion or understanding.

Disgusted at the club's handling of the situation, Jonás went on Twitter to state his feelings:

'Two things I learn from my illness: how you can support a player (newcastle fans) and how you leave a player alone (newcastle owner)'.

It would have been the easiest thing in the world to give him another year's contract. That would have been the right thing to do. But there was no testimonial; no opportunity for Jonás or Ryan to say goodbye. They were just casually cast aside. It was a brainless and also a heartless thing to do, and symptomatic of an ownership whose sole focus was trying to make money.

It always felt like regardless of what they said, the main aim of the club was to buy players cheaply from the continent and sell big, get out of the cup competitions (which weren't seen as lucrative) as early as physically possible and just remain somewhere in the 12th to 17th sort of territory in the league. Ironically, the only time they really went for it was when we went down. The small amount of credit I can give the club under Ashley was that when we were relegated – both times – we bounced straight back up, kept the players we needed and bought the best players in the Championship to give us the best possible shot. But there was always the sense that Ashley was only doing this because slipping down to the Championship was such a financial hit. Any occasional flashes of hope during his ownership were always snuffed out. We were a zombie club during his tenure – directionless, heartless and soulless.

Kevin Keegan always says to me: 'Only get involved in something you understand and have an interest in.' It was something Bobby Moore said to him after he had struggled to make any money with his ventures in hair salons and nightclubs; he then eventually bought a sports shop, which ended up doing really well for him, precisely because he was interested in it. Mike Ashley knew the high street; he didn't know how to run a football club. It was something that Alan Shearer hit the nail on the head with in a chat with me:

'I don't think he or perhaps some of his people understood the area or got the area or spent enough time in the area to get that and understand that. I'm pretty sure that he would have wanted to make it a huge success – he was a very clever man and successful businessman, but as we know, sometimes business and football are very different. He tried going in the stand in a black-and-white shirt, which I sort of understood at the beginning, but then when you're the owner of a football club, there are times that you've got to take a step back and you've got to surround yourself with the right people and take the right advice. He just never understood the football club, he never got what it was about and he never got the people, what the people wanted and how the people were, and that was his biggest mistake.'

He just didn't get it.

After multiple failed bids in his then 13-year tenure as owner of Newcastle United, a story broke in April 2020 that a bid for the club tabled by PCP Capital Partners, Reuben Brothers and the Public Investment Fund of Saudi Arabia in April 2020 was apparently at an 'advanced stage'. It was difficult to get overly excited, because the club had been through numerous attempted takeover bids. There had been Tyneside businessman Barry Moat in 2009, the 2017 bid by PCP Capital Partners, a 2019 bid by the Bin Zayed Group and, also in 2019, Peter Kenyon & GACP Sports. None of these had ever either persuaded Ashley to sell or come to fruition. Still, every day, we fans would hope and pray that someone, anyone, would buy the football club. But we wouldn't allow ourselves any measure of joy until a contract had been signed in black and white. However, this time I'd heard it was different. I'd heard the money behind this potential takeover would make it a genuine possibility. I allowed myself a small tinge of excitement inwardly, but I had no idea how many twists and turns and sleepless nights lay ahead.

CHAPTER **6**

THE **2021** TAKEOVER

It was 7 October 2021. It was a day I'll never forget, both personally and professionally. A historic moment in the history of Newcastle United. It was the end of an agonisingly long wait for United fans, who were desperate to see the back of Mike Ashley's ownership, but an agreement was finally made, 541 days after the takeover bid had been submitted by the consortium comprising PCP Capital Partners, Reuben Brothers and the Public Investment Fund of Saudi Arabia (PIF). The previous day, it had been reported that the long-running ban on Qatari media group beIN Sports (one of the Premier League's official broadcasting partners) from broadcasting in Saudi Arabia had been lifted, and perhaps that was the final obstruction as it seemed to pave the way for the deal, which looked like it had collapsed in July 2020.

Newcastle United put out a statement to announce that the investment group '… has completed the acquisition of 100 per cent of Newcastle United Limited and Newcastle United Football Club Limited from St. James Holdings Limited. All requisite approvals have been obtained from the English Premier League and the acquisition was completed on 7 October 2021.'

The Premier League also released its own statement to confirm that: 'Following the completion of the Premier League's

Owners' and Directors' Test, the club has been sold to the consortium with immediate effect ...

All parties are pleased to have concluded this process, which gives certainty and clarity to Newcastle United Football Club and their fans.'

As my colleague Keith Downie read the statements live on Sky Sports News, the outpouring of relief and joy around St James' Park and across Tyneside was absolutely overwhelming. You could hear the cheers across the city. I have to say though, most Newcastle United fans (including me) were frustrated that the celebrations were misinterpreted by large sections of the national media. These wild celebrations were less about the new owners and more about the fact that Mike Ashley was finally gone. There had been numerous failed takeover attempts over the years and there was a belief on Tyneside that the club would remain in limbo until it was sold. But now that the sale had happened, it felt like the new beginning that the supporters had been dreaming about. People thought, *Oh look, they're happy because they've suddenly got loads of money*, or whatever, but that definitely wasn't the driving force behind the joy. Yes, they welcomed the change of ownership and yes, Amanda Staveley was being hailed as the latest Messiah on Tyneside, but it was the back of Ashley that had brought the loudest cheer.

The announcement of the takeover had followed a very nervous few days for me personally. I'd received a tip-off on the previous Friday night (1 October) that the takeover had taken a significant step forward and was likely to be passed through within the next few days. I was stunned and massively excited at the same time. I decided to try and get confirmation from another source, so I messaged three or four people I knew who were close to the deal. I didn't want to be too obvious, so I just asked them if there was any update I needed to be aware of. Usually these people had been replying straight away to me, therefore I was expecting some sort of reply. But out of the four people I messaged, two didn't reply at all and the other two simply sent emojis that suggested my information was correct. One sent the zipped-mouth emoji alongside the heart emoji. The other sent the eyes-glancing-to-the-left emoji alongside the shaking-hands emoji. It was enough to confirm in my mind that this was actually happening. Mad isn't it – in this day and age, an emoji can speak a thousand words.

I suppose I could have taken a punt and had a world exclusive, but I just didn't have enough to take the gamble and if I'm honest I also felt a small responsibility as a fan. I didn't want anything to jinx a takeover that had been such a long time coming. I mean, we'd waited 540-odd days, so what difference would a couple more make? I've always got on well with the majority of people behind the scenes at the club and I have a lot of sources, so if I'm hearing a story from multiple sources, I know that something serious is taking place. I remember feeling pretty certain when I woke up on the Saturday morning that it was really going to happen early the following week. But I sat on the story until everything was done and dusted. I literally didn't tell anyone, not even my family or close mates – and my mates would have had the best weekend of their lives if I'd told them, but I more or less kept it to myself. I suppose I must have been a part of a fairly small handful of people who had an inkling what was about to happen. In the end I decided to make a call to my boss at Sky Sports News, Mark Alford, and explained the reasons behind my 'hunch'. He was really helpful and we went about making sure the Sky Sports team were ready and waiting for a potentially big story in the North East the following week, without speculating about what that story might actually be. We just had to make sure that when the announcement was made, we could be ready to lead the way.

As a fan, along with every other Geordie, I just wanted Ashley out. Fans had been dreaming of his departure for the last 14 years – and there was a feeling that nothing could move forward until he'd gone. And then it happened. My friend Keith Downie was on Sky Sports News live just after 5pm on Thursday, 7 October outside the stadium announcing: 'Finally the Newcastle United supporters have got what they have wanted for a long, long time.' The deal had been done. And with that, the black cloud over St James' Park lifted.

There were jubilant scenes on that night as thousands of fans celebrated by the statue of Sir Bobby. Local singer Sam Fender was in amongst those celebrations and he summed it up perfectly on *BBC News* the following morning when he said, 'We went straight up to St James' and my saxophone player Jonny got on the statue and started playing "Local Hero" and 5,000 Geordies just started singing along ... because Ashley's out, yeah ... I did about a thousand selfies, got proper mobbed but everyone was absolutely class and they gave us a lot of cans and I'm really hung-over, I'm really, really hung-over.'

Talking of cans, the hashtag #cans had been trending on social media that day. It was Newcastle United fans celebrating by drinking 'cans' of ale to celebrate the change of ownership at the club. It brought about one of the strangest things that has ever happened to me at work, when the receptionist at the security gate at Sky called me up and said, 'There's been a delivery here for you at the gate.' When I went down, there was a bag of ice-cold Stella Artois that a generous Newcastle United fan had ordered online and sent to the studios so I could join in the celebrations. Sadly, I was far too busy to drink them that night, but don't worry they got demolished on the train back to Newcastle the following afternoon. I remember that train journey as well. People were coming up to me and shaking my hand and hugging me. Thanking Sky Sports for the coverage. When the train finally rolled into Newcastle I got off the train and already you could feel the change in the city. It felt like a completely different place and there was a buzz in the air.

After the dust had settled, we all took more notice of the new owners, their ambitions for the club and the direction they wanted to move the club in. As for the public face of the new ownership, that was Amanda Staveley. Amanda, originally from Ripon in North Yorkshire, became a successful businesswoman in her twenties, opening a restaurant near Newmarket racetrack with a £180,000 loan in 1996. At the same time as working as a chef and waitress in her own restaurant, which had become popular with stables' owners – including wealthy Middle Eastern investors and high-tech entrepreneurs based at Cambridge Science Park, who'd been using Amanda's restaurant to host board meetings – she was also studying to become a financial adviser. Spotting a business opportunity, she set up (in partnership with Trinity College, Cambridge) Q.ton – a conference centre, restaurant and gym complex. By 2005, she'd founded the Dubai-based international private equity firm PCP Capital Partners. And three years later, she acted for Manchester City in the £210 million sale of the club to Sheikh Mansour through the Abu Dhabi United Group. She married British-Iranian businessman Mehrdad Ghodoussi, whom she'd worked with at PCP, in 2011.

Amanda fell in love with Newcastle United when she came to St James' Park in October 2017 to see us play Liverpool when Rafa Benítez was our manager. She knew that the club was for sale at that time and so went about trying to find a new owner, and that won her a lot of respect from Newcastle United fans. Less than two months later, in November 2017, she submitted a bid with her company, PCP Partners, to buy the club from Mike Ashley. That bid was rejected, but fans took a lot of hope from her involvement in a potential deal because she had an incredible track record with Man City's takeover in 2008.

The crazy thing is that my family had a big link to Amanda's family. My mum was a stable hand as a teenager and she'd look after the Staveley family horses in her spare time. She used to spend the summer holidays at Amanda's grandparents' house and she formed a close bond with Amanda's mum, Lynne – they were both from Doncaster and became close friends. I remember them often talking on the phone when I was a kid. My mum still can't believe that Amanda has, in her words, 'saved our football club' and she always says her late mum Lynne would have been immensely proud of everything Amanda has achieved.

After the deal finally went through, the first thing Amanda did was to speak to the fans who'd been celebrating outside. And after that, she spoke to Keith live on Sky Sports News and said:

'We'd first of all like to thank the incredible fans – we wouldn't be here without them today. It's their club. We want to be great custodians of this club – we take our role very very seriously … Really, genuinely, we want to invest in every area of this club at every level and we know it's at the heart of the community, you can feel that. I mean it's so touching for me as well to be able to talk about this openly.'

And from that moment on, the communication between the club and the supporters has been terrific and it's been such a welcome change from the Ashley era.

While Amanda was wary in her interview with Keith about 'overpromising', she made it clear that she wants to see Newcastle win trophies, and that she's in it for the long term because success was going to require patience, investment and time. 'We want everybody to work with us to build the club towards what it needs to be.' Most importantly, she conveyed that the owners' ambition was aligned with the supporters – the club had high hopes for the future and wanted to be something everyone was proud of again. She hit all the right notes, and she was speaking from the heart. I suppose she's considered the Queen of Newcastle's new era, and Amanda and Mehrdad are absolutely loved by the people of Newcastle. Mehrdad was appointed one of the club's directors together with Jamie Reuben, of RB Sports & Media (an offshoot of the private equity and investment firm Reuben Brothers), who had (like PCP) also acquired a 10 per cent stake in the club.

Mehrdad seemed really down to earth – I liked him instantly. He was posing for selfies with fans and talking about how he and Amanda 'were blown away' by the club after they saw their first match together back in 2017. Jamie was seen happily mingling with fans before the Spurs game on 17 October 2021 outside the stadium and both he and Mehrdad interact with fans on social media all the time. You can see how much they both love football and how much they care about the club already, so they've been welcomed with open arms by the fans.

After the euphoria of 7 October, there was a lot of work to be done. The club had been barely treading water under Ashley but the new owners had demonstrated they were in it for the long term, committing to heavy investment in the club and the city. The first item on the agenda? Finding a manager with the drive, ambition, determination and a long-term plan that matched their own.

CHAPTER 7

EDDIE HOWE – THAT **FELLA** FROM BOURNEMOUTH

The whole city celebrated the end of the Ashley era, but one place where we were a little short on the celebration front was on the pitch. Our start to the 2020–21 season was four losses and three draws from seven games. Three days after the takeover, we played our first official match under the new ownership. The owners had made the decent, dignified decision to allow Steve Bruce to stay on for his 1,000th match as manager. Bruce remaining in the dugout didn't detract from the buzz around the stadium ahead of the game. The club's new chairman, Yasir Al-Rumayyan, was introduced to the fans for the first time to an explosion of cheers and applause. Amanda, Mehrdad and Jamie were alongside him.

It felt like a historic moment for the club as Jimmy Nail's 'Big River' boomed out of the stadium PA. It was a new beginning and an emotional moment. Lifted by the incredible atmosphere United flew out of the blocks and we were ahead after just two minutes. Callum Wilson headed in the opener and the stadium roof nearly came off. But the dream start eventually slipped away and the match finished 3–2 to the visitors. Steve Bruce's days looked numbered. He was a Mike Ashley appointment and three days after that defeat to Spurs, the inevitable announcement was made. We were 19th in the table, didn't show signs of improving and, as Steve himself admitted, 'New owners normally want a new manager. I've been around long enough to understand that.'

Unai Emery, the then Villarreal manager and former Valencia, Sevilla, PSG and Arsenal boss, who had won three Europa League titles in a row with Sevilla from 2014–16, along with the Ligue 1 title and four domestic cups with PSG, became the front-runner for the job. We actually broke the story on Sky Sports News that Newcastle United was close to appointing him. It kind of came out of the blue to us at Sky, but a big name from the continent made sense to the fans given what we imagined the new owners might have been aiming for. The problem was that the story emerged the night that Villarreal were playing in the Champions League at home against Young Boys (a game Villarreal won 2–0), and the fans were all chanting his name. I think Emery must have panicked after that and began to stall. Eventually, he turned down the offer. Here's what he had to say in April the following year to The Athletic about why he chose to stay put at Villarreal:

'I thought about the offer and I spoke with [Villarreal president] Fernando Roig, but I also had to take into account that we were in the Champions League with Villarreal, mid-season. In the end, with a lot of respect for Villarreal, and a lot of respect for Newcastle, I decided to stay here. I am happy here and we are doing an important job.'

In fairness to Emery, the previous year he had lifted the Europa League trophy with Villarreal in the final in May 2021, defeating Man United 11–10 in an epic penalty shootout that came down to the Villarreal keeper scoring his pen and David de Gea missing his. It was the first time the club had ever won the trophy and so they qualified for the group stages of the Champions League for the first time in a decade, and they made it to the semi-finals, beating Juventus and Bayern Munich along the way before being stopped by Liverpool. He was a hero there at the time and it made sense they wouldn't want to lose him.

Just three days after we broke the Emery story, on 5 November, the club had agreed a deal in principle with Eddie Howe. My under-standing was that Eddie had really impressed the owners, and that it had almost come down to the flip of a coin between him and Emery, and the reports had got ahead of themselves. Personally, I was over the moon that it was Eddie Howe. I always had respect for him, the job he did at Bournemouth and the style of football he played. Also, things that players had told me or I'd heard them say about Eddie had stuck in my mind. One of them was Jack Wilshere, talking on the radio, and the presenter did a quiz with him about the managers he'd played for. Bear in mind that Jack had played for some of the biggest managers around: Wenger, Capello, Pellegrini, Moyes, Hodgson, and he played for Eddie Howe while on loan from Arsenal in 2016–17. The presenter was asking him who the best man manager, tactician, trainer etc. was and a lot of the answers Jack gave were Eddie Howe. And that surprised me, because Wilshere only played 20-odd games for the club in a team that was struggling. That was when I started to wonder if there was something really special about Eddie as a manager.

I said to my mates at the time: 'This is the one, lads,' and they were all rolling their eyes because apparently, I say that about

everyone. And of course, while I batted them away, there is probably an element of truth behind it. I like to get behind the manager
when they're brought in. But I do remember thinking at the time
that Eddie Howe would be a really good fit for our football club.
He was young, dynamic and full of ideas, and at the same time
he seemed calm, measured, wise ahead of his years, and people
respected him. I know it's easy to say all that now. But when he
joined, the fans weren't universally behind him.

When Steve Bruce had been asked about Eddie Howe's links
to the club the previous January, he'd replied to the reporter, saying,
'The fella from Bournemouth who got a team relegated?' This quote
doesn't look great for Bruce now of course. However, I imagine there
were a handful of supporters who were on the fence initially about
Howe's arrival. That's normal with any new managerial appointment. This was certainly a step up for Howe, with all due respect to
his previous clubs, and there was a sense of intrigue surrounding how
he would get on managing a club with so much potential. Howe had
worked wonders with a small club punching above its weight until
they finally lost momentum. But this was Newcastle United we were
talking about. So who was this guy and what could he offer us?

Eddie Howe was born in Buckinghamshire but had relocated
to the little town of Verwood in Dorset as a young lad after his
parents separated. It was just 10 miles north of Bournemouth and
so Eddie grew up as an AFC Bournemouth fan, kicking a football
by the garages around the back of his house with his half-brother
Peter Lovell. They'd draw a goal on the wall and stay out for hours
playing football together.

Eddie was also a really good cricketer, opening the batting for the local village cricket team, and making it to county level. However, when it came down to a choice between football and cricket, there was only ever going to be one winner. Football was both his passion and his priority. Eddie started his football career as a 13-year-old at community-based team Phoenix FC, just north of Bournemouth, joining several promising players from his own street, before going to local team Rossgarth Youth FC (now Verwood Town). And then, one day – 'out of the blue' as Eddie says – he was given a business card by a Bournemouth scout, inviting him to come and train with them at the AFC Bournemouth Centre of Excellence.

Eddie went on to captain the Cherries Youth team before making his first-team debut – at 18 years old – in a Second Division league win against Hull City at Dean Court in December 1995. He won the Man of the Match award for that game, made two more appearances that season and earned himself a professional contract with the club in the summer of 1996. He became a vital central defender for the club and a fan favourite in the next couple of seasons.

The 1997–98 season turned out to be a big one for the 20-year-old Howe, as he dislocated his kneecap in February but recovered quickly and was named Player of the Season. He got his first taste of a final at Wembley – the 1997–98 Auto Windscreens Shield (also known as the Football League Trophy). Unfortunately, they lost, agonisingly, to a 112th-minute golden goal (remember those?!) against Grimsby. But that was when he got the best news of his career up to that date: England came calling. Eddie was modest about it when talking to Jamie Carragher on Sky Sports: 'I had no idea that England even knew my name but I got called up for the Toulon Tournament.* We had a few pull-outs, so they looked deeper into the lower leagues. I got a call-up, along with Jamie [Carragher] and Frank Lampard and some other great players. It was just a great experience for me.'

In 2002, Eddie was signed by new Portsmouth boss Harry Redknapp for £400,000. Fellow Pompey defender Linvoy Primus was complimentary about what Eddie brought to the club: '... it was clear to all of us that he was exactly the kind of player we needed. He played the game like he acted – he was very composed, a really classy centre-back.'

Eddie was Harry's first signing at the club but it didn't start well for the new player, going down with a knee injury during his debut away against Preston North End in March. It ended Eddie's season.

After recovering from that major setback, disaster struck again. It was only Eddie's second game for the club – on the first day of the 2002–03 season against Nottingham Forest – but Eddie would play no part in it, suffering a recurrence of the knee problem. It ruled him out for the entire 2002–03 season and a fair chunk of the next one. I can't even imagine the frustration he

---

* The Toulon Tournament is a national competition featuring players from U-17 to U-23 level. The 1998 tournament was the 26th edition, featuring France, Argentina, Brazil, China, England, Germany, Portugal and South Africa.

must have felt after getting back to full fitness only to find himself on the sidelines watching a squad that featured Shaka Hislop, Paul Merson, Steve Stone, Yakubu and Tim Sherwood go on to win the First Division title that year under Harry Redknapp.

That Forest game would be the last appearance he made for Portsmouth, and he was loaned to Swindon Town in March 2004 and then Bournemouth in August 2004. His loan move back to Bournemouth became permanent after five months, albeit in slightly unconventional fashion. The club couldn't afford to buy Howe as their finances were at rock bottom, but a group of Bournemouth fans set up a platform they called 'Eddieshare', raising funds through crowdfunding to bring their favourite son back home. The plan succeeded and Eddie was moved by the response of the fans, telling the *Bournemouth Daily Echo*: 'I thought it was an incredible gesture, one that made me feel very attached again to the club, very emotional and my aim then was to try and repay their faith.' Eddie made another 50 starts for Bournemouth but his knee had never recovered. In a 2–0 away loss at Crewe after which Eddie acknowledged he'd performed terribly and felt like he'd let the team down, Eddie knew the time had come and he told then manager Kevin Bond it would be his final game. He was just 29.

Just a few days later, Kevin Bond offered Eddie an opportunity. There was a game coming up and Kevin needed someone to scout out the opposition. This offer came at a good time for Eddie, because he'd known for a while that his playing career was going to be cut short, so it had forced him to look at football differently and start considering other ways of finding a job still within the game. So when Kevin asked Eddie if he'd be interested, he said yes, there and then. Eddie wrote a report, gave it to Kevin, and the Bournemouth side went on and won the game. After that, Kevin asked Eddie to become part of his coaching team, taking charge of their reserves in early 2007, which he accepted.

Bond was sacked by the club after a disappointing start to the 2008–09 season, following relegation from League One the previous season (though they'd also started the 2008–09 season on –17 points after they had failed to exit administration). Both Eddie Howe and Bond's assistant manager, Rob Newman, were also let go. But it wasn't to be a long spell out of coaching for Eddie – he was re-hired a week later by the club to take charge of the club's centre for excellence, coaching the 8- to 16-year-olds there.

Kevin Bond's replacement, Jimmy Quinn, was hired in September 2008 but after just 121 days, with the club second from bottom of League Two and seven points adrift of safety, he was sacked too. And that's when Eddie got a fateful call, on New Year's Eve in 2008, while he was at a party hosted by former Portsmouth player Richard Hughes. It was from Adam Murry, who was at the time trying to put together a consortium to rescue the club. Murry asked Eddie to sit in the hot seat for the first time, taking over as caretaker boss. It wasn't an appointment that all of the fans welcomed, though. One of them had turned up at Murry's house and sprayed 'You don't know what you're doing' on his wall.

Eddie went about his task straight away the next morning, New Year's Day 2009. My mate and colleague Mark McAdam, who was working at Bournemouth back then, remembers going round to Howe's that day. He told the Sky Sports website: 'He didn't have coaching staff, recruitment staff, anything at all. There were flip charts all over the place, lists of players, scouting reports … He walked into an environment where he had nothing. He had to build it himself, create an identity, create an atmosphere in the dressing room, sign players with the right characteristics … He'd pay the masseuses out of his money because the club couldn't afford to have a masseuse for the day.'

Eddie told Murry he wanted Quinn's assistant manager – Eddie's former teammate at Bournemouth, Jason Tindall – to stay on. Eddie admitted they didn't really know each other, beyond a mutual respect, but the partnership clicked straight away and they've never looked back. Unfortunately for this new partnership, the next two fixtures in the calendar were both tricky away games, which they lost. Shortly after that, in mid-January 2009, Eddie got another call from Murry. When he saw the name flash up on his phone, Eddie was convinced he'd be getting the sack again, but Murry was actually calling him to offer him the job permanently. It caught Eddie by surprise. In an interview with The Coaches' Voice, Eddie said: 'I thought he was mad! I tried to get him to change his mind and say no no no, you need someone else, but he was adamant.'

To be fair, it was a massive gamble from Murry, giving the reins to an untested 31-year-old manager – the youngest manager in the entire league – who hadn't even won a game yet. As for Eddie, his task was clear: pull off the great escape. The club faced relegation from the Football League. And for a club already suffering severe financial problems, that would have been the end of AFC Bournemouth.

· · ·

Eddie's first game as manager wasn't the ideal fixture either, against table-topping Wycombe Wanderers, but, after going behind courtesy of a back-pass cock-up, to the delight of Cherries' fans Bournemouth won the game 3–1 at home in front of their biggest crowd of the season so far. Draws against fellow strugglers Luton Town and mid-table Lincoln City followed before wins on the bounce at home to play-off hopefuls Shrewsbury Town and Accrington Stanley. And all the time, they were battling adversity both on and off the pitch. Their squad was so depleted that Eddie's assistant, right-hand man and brother-in-arms Jason Tindall – a retired defender – was named as a sub against Dagenham and Redbridge away. He even had to come on in the 69th minute. And it's a good job he did because he set up Mark Molesley in the final minute to win the game for them. Actually 'set up' might be a little generous. Steve Hard, the Bournemouth physio said: '... technically he just booted it out of the penalty area like a John Smith's advert.' But he did a job that day for his gaffer, that's for sure. That was Eddie's first away win.

On the penultimate day of the season, against Grimsby Town at home, a win would secure their survival as a Football League club. Well, Bournemouth rose to the occasion, winning the game 2–1, with their talismanic frontman Steve Fletcher – a club legend who became Eddie's first signing, bringing him back to Bournemouth from Crawley Town – scoring the winner.

While Eddie was relieved and delighted at the final whistle, telling Sky Sports in a post-match interview that 'you couldn't write it', what came across was not only confidence and composure but also intellect, hunger and a long-term vision. Here's what he said towards the end of the interview: 'The hard work starts now really for us. We want to build a team that can hopefully challenge at the top end of the table for next year. It should be a lot of hard work, but for tonight we'll enjoy this one.' Although they couldn't enjoy it that much – the club was so strapped for cash that they sprayed water rather than champagne at the end of the game.

Bournemouth finished the season on 46 points, which is all the more impressive when you consider the –17 point deduction, the three managerial changes, a poor start to the season and the quite unbelievable tales that were coming out of a club on the verge of liquidation. Apparently, the players weren't even getting paid for some of the season. They received their wages for February at the end of March thanks to a loan from the PFA, and some of the total wage bill had arrived – in cash – at the home dressing room in an M&S carrier bag. Bailiffs were even removing stock from the club shop and, to avoid humiliation, the staff came up with the novel idea of taking down some of the roof tiles to 'create' a water leak, so they could explain to supporters why the shelves at the club shop were empty. Training sessions were moved to local parks after the gates at the training ground were found with padlocks on them. Players were literally picking up dog sh*t so they could play on the park's pitches.

Nonetheless, they had undeniably done very well that season. Without the deduction, they would have finished in 10th, only six points short of the play-offs. Attendances skyrocketed at Dean Court in the final two home games, topping 9,000 against Grimsby, and they finished the season with three wins on the trot, including thumping Morecambe 4–0 away on the final day of the season.

Under the circumstances, Eddie had pulled off nothing short of a miracle. But how on earth had he managed to mastermind the great escape?

Eddie's work ethic from his first day as manager was second to none, and it's something he feels he owes to his late mother. Raising five kids on her own, she worked three jobs to make ends meet. She'd often take one or two of her kids to the job at the newsagent that began around 4am, so Eddie grew up used to early starts. Her commitment and dedication rubbed off on Eddie. And so he started his management career making it to training by 6am. He was the first into the training ground and the last person off the training pitch at the end of a session. He led by example.

Eddie is generous with his praise for his former manager, Sean O'Driscoll (Bournemouth's manager from 2000 to 2006). The two of them went back to the early 1990s, when Eddie was a youth team player and O'Driscoll was a senior pro. O'Driscoll was, in some respects, a pioneer of a football manager. He was a manager full of new ideas with a strong emphasis on individual improvement. He didn't want his players to become robots, going through the motions that their manager would dictate to them. It was all part of a philosophy of wanting his players to think more about what they were doing both on and off the pitch. As part of this, he'd openly invite his players to both question him and conventional footballing wisdom during training sessions. It was something O'Driscoll started as a player, which he admits used to drive Harry Redknapp (O'Driscoll's manager at the time) up the wall.

One example of O'Driscoll's methods was, rather than gathering the entire squad around to speak to them about a particular drill (as was common practice at the time), he'd divide the group up into two teams, explain the rules to just one player from each team and ask them to relay it to their team. It was a clever way of working on his players' ability to communicate with their teammates, while he could monitor that they'd fully understood the instructions he'd given them. It was all geared towards maximising their performance when it came to a proper match, because in that situation you can't gather your squad around and relay instructions to them – you relay messages to a player closest to you near the dugout or a substitute who's coming on. Similarly, unlike almost every football manager from that era, O'Driscoll wouldn't shout at his players if they had a poor game or if the team lost. Instead, he asked them to deconstruct their own performance. He had a keen interest in mental training inspired by Dr Steve Peters, the sports psychologist, who was already by that time having a big impact on the British Cycling team.

O'Driscoll's methods had a powerful impact on Eddie Howe while he was playing at Bournemouth. And when he moved to Portsmouth, only to suffer through injury, he spent the best part of two seasons mostly by himself, watching Harry Redknapp and his assistant manager Jim Smith turn a team battling to stay in the then First Division in the 2001–02 season into champions in 2002–03. He'd had a remarkable football education watching two completely different coaches, both of whom had taken their teams up a league. He'd also had to cope with the isolation of long-term injury, which he told The Coaches' Voice in 2020 meant that he'd started to look 'at alternative ways to find employment in the game'. His strong work ethic continued while he was out injured – ever hungry to learn, he was absorbing new ways to train and to think. He'd started his coaching journey long before he'd become a coach. In some ways, it allowed him to hit the ground running, even if it didn't feel that way to him at the time.

Another reason for Eddie's success in that first season is the warrior mentality he had no choice but to forge. Not only were Bournemouth completely strapped for cash, they were also under a transfer embargo as part of the punishment for going into admin-istration. It galvanised something in Eddie, forcing him to develop the resourcefulness to work with what he had. And that became one of the most important lessons he learned and it helped to shape him as a manager. He learned to adapt to adversity. But even more than that, both management and the players were bonded together, united by the feeling of injustice at the situation they found themselves in. It fostered a unique team spirit.

. . .

However, despite Eddie's optimism for the 2009–10 season, the club was still in dire straits financially. A new chairman – Eddie

Mitchell, a local property developer – took over, but the club was facing historic debts and a squad numbering fewer than 20 players. Promotion the following season was a pipe dream, especially as they would be under a transfer embargo for most of the upcoming season as well. Eddie had dealt with a stern test the previous season and secured their survival, but this was a completely different challenge. He'd have to pivot from the back foot to the front foot.

It was around about this time that Eddie was first introduced to the work of John Wooden, the legendary coach of the UCLA Bruins in California. Eddie recalls being given one of Wooden's books from a friend soon after he became Bournemouth manager. Wooden's inspirational teachings went beyond sports and into leadership, success and personal development, and Eddie credits him with transforming his approach to management and coaching. John Wooden quotes appeared around Eddie's office at Bournemouth and he turned to Wooden when he needed an uplifting message. Wooden's impact also awoke a desire to broaden his horizons and seek inspiration not only within football.

Inspired by Wooden's work, Eddie began to focus on tailoring how to work on the weaknesses of every single player in his squad. He made it his mission to get to know each and every one of them and to learn how to bring the best out of them. And all the while, he was adapting to difficulties that came along, including the fact that the small size of the squad meant that he was forced to field his players out of their usual positions and to ask them to play when they were injured.

Straight out of the gates for the 2009–10 season, they beat Bury 3–0 away before facing a test against promotion chasers Rotherham United at Dean Court and coming out 1–0 winners. Three days later, they maintained their 100 per cent start to the season with another 1–0 win, against Aldershot at home. This meant they'd won eight of their first nine games. By Christmas they were second in League Two and suddenly the pipe dream was becoming real. Three successive defeats at the turn of 2010 threatened to burst the bubble, but a tricky away win at Crewe Alexandra stopped the brief rot. Two wins in a row in April put them on the verge of securing automatic promotion if they could beat Burton Albion away at the Pirelli Stadium the next week. Goals from top scorer Brett Pitman and a last-minute goal from Alan Connell were the cherries on the top of a fairy-tale season. It simply should not have been possible, but Eddie found a way. Much like Kevin Keegan at Newcastle in 1991–92, Eddie Howe had saved Bournemouth from an unthinkable drop before leading them to promotion the following season. Eddie had also done it with absolutely zero help or support from above. It was an incredible achievement.

The 2010–11 season began with excitement despite an opening-day loss to promotion hopefuls Charlton Athletic. Eddie really announced that Bournemouth meant business in the second game of the season, a 5–1 rout against Peterborough United with a Pitman hat-trick sending Dean Court wild. Most clubs who get promoted set their sights at surviving the following season, but Eddie set his sights high and inspired the same outlook in his players. He was developing a reputation as the most exciting young coach in the entire Football League, and as such, big clubs in the top divisions were taking notice.

Among them was Championship side Burnley, who'd been relegated from the Premier League the previous season. Just after Christmas 2011, Burnley were sitting in eighth place in the table and had lost three of their past five – not the sort of form the owners, who wanted to bounce straight back to the Premier League, were after. So they sacked manager Brian Laws and courted Eddie Howe as his replacement. In the end, Burnley proved to be too tempting a proposition. The owners had a very clear vision that would have appealed to the ambitious, hungry Howe: get Burnley back into the Premier League.

Eddie didn't deliver what the owners wanted, with the club finishing in eighth at the end of the season. And the following season didn't start well either, with only one win in seven games – the kind of form that tends to send managers packing these days. But a thumping 5–1 win at Nottingham Forest happened at just the right time, followed by an away victory at Millwall. The rest of the season was chequered with promising periods and then winless streaks, but the board kept faith with Eddie.

In the end, he stayed at Burnley until October 2012. He'd been struggling with a personal tragedy for several months – his mum, Anne, died after a short illness in March that year. He said of that time: 'I didn't have any time to grieve. You're straight back to work as a manager, you're managing from seven in the morning until seven at night, but you've got all these emotions running through you.' An opportunity had arisen at his old club, Bournemouth, after manager Paul Groves had been let go. Eddie, keen to return down south for personal reasons, was offered the job, and he took it. When he returned, the club was sitting in 21st place in League One, registering only one win in the first 11 games.

Eddie's impact was instantaneous, winning six out of the next seven games and going unbeaten in 15. It was a stunning comeback, again. Only this time the club was in better shape financially and Eddie had more freedom in the transfer market. He made that count straight away with a very smart loan deal in November 2012 for Brett Pitman, who rejoined the club (and reunited with his former manager) from Bristol City. The 24-year-old repaid his new manager by scoring in his first game, equalising in the final minute after coming on as a substitute. Eddie had made the loan a three-and-a-half-year deal during the January transfer window and it proved to be a master stroke. Pitman scored 20 goals that season – quite some return given that he only joined them a third of the way through the season. Eddie also brought in 18-year-old Ryan Fraser from Aberdeen and 23-year-old Matt Ritchie, both of whom would go on to play under Eddie at Newcastle. Eddie was proving he could spend wisely when money was available, investing in promising young players who went on to prove their worth to the club.

Eddie weathered a five-game losing streak in February and March, but hit back with an incredible string of eight wins, the last of which secured Bournemouth automatic promotion to the Championship. They were a whisker away from winning the league – a final-day victory would have done it, but they settled for second, not that that really mattered. They were in dreamland. Eddie had led them to two promotions in three years, and of course, Eddie now had his sights on the Premier League.

The huge excitement for the 2014–15 season started over the summer with the announcement that the Cherries would play Real Madrid in a friendly in July 2013 at the Goldsands Stadium.* Eddie hailed it for all the positives: 'These are good days for the club and hopefully everyone will enjoy this year because it is rare this club has ever played at this level, so everything is positive.' The side of the All Stars, featuring Luka Modrić, Mesut Özil, Sami Khedira, Gonzalo Higuaín, Ángel Di María and Cristiano Ronaldo ran out 6–0 winners in front of a sell-out crowd of 12,000, but it's testament to Eddie's attitude that the players were disappointed afterwards, having more than held their own for the opening 20 minutes. That wasn't the only brush with Champions League winners that season, though. They hosted Liverpool in the fourth round of the FA Cup at Dean Court and matched them for long stretches of the game, before Luis Suárez turned provider twice to help Liverpool to a 2–0 win. They finished 10th in the league that season – a strong mid-table finish in their first season in the Championship, and that gave them a foundation to build from.

Over the summer, Eddie made another terrific young signing – 22-year-old Callum Wilson from Coventry City. Wilson hit the ground running, having no problem adapting to the

* Dean Court had become the Goldsands Stadium in February 2012 in a two-year sponsorship deal.

Championship after spending the previous season banging in 22 goals in League One. Wilson warmed up nicely with a hat-trick in the final pre-season friendly against Oxford United, before making his full debut in the first game of the season – scoring twice in a rampant 4–0 win against Huddersfield Town. It would have been a second hat-trick in two games were it not for a good save by keeper Alex Smithies. Eddie also brought in Junior Stanislas on a three-year deal in June 2014, which, given the fact that Stanislas was about to play in the Premier League, having helped Burnley to promotion in 2013–14, showed how much he prized reuniting with his old boss. Stanislas told the *Lancashire Telegraph*: 'He always had faith in me and stuck with me … so when I knew Bournemouth were interested, with Eddie Howe as manager, I really wanted to come down here and work with him again.'

The 2014–15 season actually started pretty modestly after that 4–0 away win on the opening day. There was a narrow 1–0 home win against a strong Brentford side, with Eddie's new signing Stanislas proving the difference between the two sides, which gave them two wins in two, before an old-fashioned smash and grab from Nottingham Forest in the next game robbed Bournemouth of a win they should have wrapped up by half-time. Eddie was dumbfounded: 'I don't know how to explain that. It was one of the strangest games I have been involved in,' he said to the press afterwards. But it was to be the start of a tricky period for the Cherries, facing some of the big guns in the division in Norwich City, Blackburn Rovers and Watford. They only managed three points from the next six games, and it was a sobering time.

After eight games, they'd amassed nine points, which was hardly promotion-chasing form.

At this time, Eddie had his eye on Poland international keeper Artur Boruc, Southampton's first-choice keeper the previous season and whose position as number one had been recently taken over by Fraser Forster. Eddie explained that he wanted to increase competition in the goalkeeping department and wanted a strong shot-stopper with a great deal of experience at the highest level. Boruc, who'd been capped nearly 60 times by his country, joined on 19 September on an emergency short-term loan and it proved to be a great move for the player and the club.

In October, Eddie had managed to turn the team's form around. An away win at Bolton, despite going down to 10 men at the end of the first half, showed real grit. Eddie said afterwards, in a quote that would foreshadow his famous quote while Newcastle manager: 'That should give us a huge lift for the remaining games that we have this season that we can compete.' That performance gave them the confidence to push on. A win at home to Charlton thanks to an early Wilson strike built up the momentum, and then they started to move up the gears. A dominant 3–0 win at home to Reading was followed by a quite extraordinary display against Birmingham City, obliterating them 8–0. It was record-breaking for both clubs – the first time Bournemouth had scored eight in a league game,* their biggest winning margin in the league, and Birmingham's heaviest home defeat. They had a man sent

---

* The 10–0 win in 1939 against Northampton Town had been removed from the record books with World War II breaking out the next day.

off within seven minutes, but Bournemouth were already 1–0 up by then anyway, before putting them to the sword in the second half. Birmingham's one glimmer of hope was snuffed out by a fantastic Boruc penalty save. It was a statement win and moved Bournemouth into the play-off places. A 3–2 win at home to Brighton sent them into second in the table – their sixth win in a row in all competitions. By the end of the year, they were unbeaten in 14 league games, winning 11 of them. And in those 14 games, they'd scored a scarcely believable 40 goals, putting five past Cardiff City and hitting Blackpool for six. They were top of the table at the beginning of 2015, four points clear of Ipswich Town. Could they keep this run up?

A five-game winless run in February 2015 put the champagne back in the fridge – they were still in the play-off places, but the pack was chasing. The script for the last dozen games was written in the stars, though. They were back to their imperious best, demolishing Fulham 5–1, Blackpool 4–0 and Middlesbrough 3–0. Bournemouth under Eddie Howe just didn't let up. Howe's pairing of Wilson and Pitman was absolutely on fire. All of his signings were producing their best football at the right time. And on 27 April 2015, they blew Bolton away 3–0, although it could have been a cricket score with their 24 shots, 10 of them on target. They'd suddenly sealed a simply staggering achievement. They'd made it to the Premier League. Fans were singing the *Match of the Day* theme tune at the Goldsands Stadium. The club that had been minutes away from liquidation in 2008 and just a game away from dropping out of the Football League in 2009 were on the verge of a £100 million payday and a spot in the big league. On the final day of the 2014–15 season, they put the icing on the cake, securing the Championship title with an emphatic 3–0 win away at Charlton Athletic after Watford could only draw their match against Sheffield Wednesday.

Tellingly, just 48 hours after that match, Eddie was already focused on the next season. And he intended to do it with the group of players he'd taken up from the Championship. Here's what he said to the press: 'I don't believe in wholesale changes in the close season, I don't believe in not giving players a chance to show whether they are good enough. Ultimately, they will have to take that opportunity but it was the same from League One to the Championship – we stuck with the majority of the squad.'

Eddie was rewarded for his incredible achievement by being named the League Managers Association Manager of the Year. LMA Chairman Howard Wilkinson said, announcing the award: 'Bournemouth's achievements this season are nothing short of fantastic. To take his club, which was experiencing such difficulties just a short while ago, to the Barclays Premier League required a monumental effort and everyone connected with the club during this period must be congratulated.'

It was the first time since 2006 that a manager from outside the Premier League had won the award. It wasn't the only big managerial award Eddie had won that year. He'd also been named 'Football League Manager of the Decade' at the 10th annual Football League awards ceremony towards the end of April 2015, just two games away from reaching the Premier League. Bearing in mind that Eddie had only been in management for six years, that was some achievement and a justified validation of his ability as a manager.

. . .

Eddie made a few big signings over the summer of 2015, the biggest of which was probably Tyrone Mings, who joined from Ipswich for a club record £8 million. It was a bit of a coup, as Bournemouth weren't the only club interested in recruiting the 22-year-old defender. Newcastle United, Aston Villa and West Brom were all in the running, but much of the reason was down to Eddie himself, as Mings told Sky Sports: 'The manager Eddie Howe had a big impact in me coming here – he is one of the most exciting young English managers. To come down and learn from him, and new things tactically, is only going to benefit me. Their style of play is different to any other side in the league and that tracks back to Eddie.' Forward Josh King also joined, for £1 million, from Blackburn. While his decision was partly motivated by the appeal of playing in the Premier League for the first time in his career, Eddie's appeal also had a big part to play, the player telling AFC Bournemouth's website: 'If I do get my chance in the Premier League it will be my first so that played a big factor [in my decision], but the manager was a bit more important. I've seen what he's done with the squad here … He loves the style I play and he actually thinks I can fit in with the team that's done brilliantly in the Championship.'

That period between the 2014–15 and 2015–16 seasons wasn't just about new signings for Eddie. It was also a summer of self-improvement. He travelled to football clubs across Europe to increase his knowledge, sharpen his tactical game and develop new training methods. In particular, he'd been studying Empoli, the newly promoted Serie A team managed by Maurizio Sarri (later the Napoli, Chelsea and Juventus manager) and asked if he could go and watch him work. Sarri agreed, so Eddie travelled to Italy and said of the time he spent there: 'What I saw, I was hugely impressed by and learned a lot from that experience.'

He also flew to Spain to watch Athletic Bilbao's coach Ernesto Valverde prepare for the last game of their season in La Liga, which they won 4–0 and qualified for the Europa League. They'd already made it to the Copa del Rey final, losing to a Barcelona team whose front line then comprised Messi, Suárez and Neymar (also known as MSN). What Empoli and Athletic Bilbao both shared was that they were relatively small clubs who punched above their weight given their limited resources and reliance on home-grown talent. It also gave Eddie the chance to scout players and forge connections with clubs on a similar trajectory to Bournemouth. All very smart moves.

The 2015–16 season turned out to be one of firsts. First game in the Premier League, first trip to Anfield in the Premier League – every week was being written into the Bournemouth history books. Eddie had to wait for the third game of the season for one of his players to hit the back of the net, but it was worth it, because that game against West Ham was a seven-goal thriller. Callum Wilson delivered for Eddie again, scoring a hat-trick, and in so doing, making history again for Bournemouth. He also made personal history, because his first goal in that fixture meant Wilson had scored in the Conference, League One, the Championship and Premier League, and he was only 23. But the joy was short-lived – after scoring five times in six games, Wilson ruptured his anterior cruciate ligament (ACL) against Stoke City in September, ruling him out for six months. Bournemouth now had to survive their first season in the Premier League without their top goalscorer. This had been the third serious ACL injury in his squad since the beginning of the season after big new signings Tyrone Mings and Max Gradel both went down injured in the same game on 29 August against Leicester. To a tactician like Eddie, who built his strategy around attacking opponents at pace, losing three of your quickest players was a massive setback. In fact, it must have felt to Eddie almost like the 2008–09 season when he was starting the season on minus points. Still, Eddie was no stranger to adversity – he'd built his reputation on it.

It was a tough season, with some difficult storms to weather, especially during October when they shipped 12 goals in three games, but Eddie's boys held their own, pulling off some impressive wins later in the season away at Chelsea, at home against Man United and away at our very own Newcastle United. Despite a poor end to the season, with four losses in five games (albeit tough games along the way against Liverpool, Chelsea and Man United), they made it over the 40-point threshold, which was enough for 16th, two points clear of relegation. Seeing as newly promoted Premier League teams have around a 40 per cent chance of being relegated in their first season, survival is some achievement.

Eddie made some shrewd moves in the transfer market over the summer of 2016, bringing in Nathan Aké from Chelsea and taking a chance on Jack Wilshere (whose career had been dogged by injury), both on loan deals. Wilshere impressed in the time he was at Bournemouth, winning the club's Player of the Month award in both November and December 2016, but the story was a familiar one: he suffered another injury and was ruled out for the rest of the season in April, and so returned to Arsenal. Some of Eddie's transfers didn't pan out. Jordon Ibe, the club's £15 million record signing in July 2016, had a reasonable start but found himself on the bench from October. More players left the club in the transfer window than joined, including Matt Ritchie, whom Eddie would later link up with after he became Newcastle boss.

Two defeats to Man United at home and West Ham away were followed by a draw at Crystal Palace and then a much-needed win at home to West Brom, with Callum Wilson finding the net with a fantastic flick – his first goal for nearly a year after his knee ligament injury. A 4–0 loss to Man City at the Etihad is about par for the course, but Eddie bounced back with a good home win against Everton and a 2–2 draw away at Watford. At home against Hull City, they earned their third consecutive home win, but this one was a little different. After being pegged back to 1–1 towards the end of the first half, Bournemouth rallied superbly, with a Cook header followed by a Stanislas penalty sending them into the dressing room 3–1 up. It turned into a rout in the last 10 minutes, with Wilson and Dan Gosling both finding the net and wrapping up a 6–1 win – Bournemouth's biggest victory in the Premier League to that point. But that wasn't even the highlight of their second season in the Premier League – that came against Liverpool in early December 2016, where Bournemouth staged a sensational turnaround from 2–0 down at the break to record a 4–3 win. It was Eddie's inspired substitution that turned the game, bringing on Ryan Fraser in the 55th minute. Just a minute later, Fraser made a surging run into the penalty area and was too quick for James Milner, who brought him down. Callum Wilson made no mistake from the spot. Fraser then scored himself, curling it into the corner from just inside the box on 76 minutes. And two minutes after that, he provided the cross for Steve Cook to poke home in the 78th minute. Back to 3–3. And then Nathan Aké sparked pandemonium at the Vitality Stadium with almost the last kick of the game. 'We never gave up,' Eddie said proudly afterwards, crediting his players with the stunning comeback.

It was that same belief that they could cut it with the best in the league that propelled them to a 2–2 draw at Anfield in the return fixture, with Josh King scoring a late equaliser to earn Bournemouth their first ever point away at Liverpool. They bounced back from a horrible run in February with a battling 1–1 draw at Old Trafford in early March, having gone down to 10 men at the end of the first half. Boruc was immense in that game, saving a penalty from Ibrahimović and keeping United at bay for the whole of the second half. Two wins followed, including a 3–2 win at home against West Ham, with King completing his hat-trick in the 90th minute.

Eddie won his first Premier League Manager of the Month award that month, and it was a fitting reward for the resilience and determination he'd shown to lead the club out of an eight-match winless run and clear of the relegation dogfight. Eddie's attitude was that they'd been through worse before – facing relegation and possible liquidation and losing five games in a row which bumped them out of the play-off places in March 2013. For such a young manager – Eddie wasn't even 40 before the end of the 2016–17 season – he'd faced hard times before, but he'd found a way to pick himself up off the canvas, steady himself and land some punches.

They finished the season unbeaten in five games, winning three of them, including a 4–0 thumping at home against Middlesbrough. They ended the season in ninth place, another seriously impressive performance, having only come up the season before last. Josh King had proved his worth, scoring 16 times and some at critical times in matches.

The summer dip into the transfer market was done and dusted by the end of 4 July for Eddie. Nathan Aké, who'd proved his quality during the loan deal from Chelsea, joined the club permanently for £20 million, smashing Bournemouth's transfer record. 'I had a great time last season, so I'm really happy to be back. The fans haven't seen the best of me yet.' Aké told the BBC, adding to AFC Bournemouth's YouTube channel: '… I spoke to Eddie and he gave me a lot of confidence … I think we are both similar, we like to work hard and I think the connection was there, so after that I decided almost straight away that I wanted to come here.' Asmir Begović joined on the same day as Aké, for

£10 million, also from Chelsea, and took the number 1 shirt. Jermain Defoe also signed from Sunderland, a Cherries favourite who had memorably scored in 10 consecutive games during a loan spell at Bournemouth in 2000–01 when he was only 18.

Despite having spent so big, the 2017–18 season started poorly for Bournemouth, with four successive losses, although one of them was an encouraging 2–1 home loss to Man City, which could have very easily been a win had King slotted either side of keeper Ederson in the last minute before Sterling's deflected shot moments later took the points for City. Eventually, Defoe scored the winner against Brighton – his first goal for the club since his loan spell – in the middle of September, securing the Cherries their first win of the season. Wilson finally returned from injury and started against Newcastle on 4 November 2017, in a 1–0 away win for Bournemouth. But he was firing on all cylinders in the next game, at home to Huddersfield, completing a sensational hat-trick in the 84th minute in a rampant 4–0 win – all the more impressive when you consider that Bournemouth were down to 10 men for half the game. November and most of December were lean on the results front until a Boxing Day feast of a match against West Ham produced a 3–3 draw, with Bournemouth 2–1 up until the 81st minute, and 3–2 down by the 89th minute, until Wilson nodded an Aké cross in in the last minute.

That would then prove to be the platform for a strong run of results, going seven games unbeaten including a 2–1 home win against Arsenal, Wilson again on the scoresheet, and an inspired 3–0 away win at Stamford Bridge. Eddie hailed the latter as their best result in the Premier League and it was a tactical masterclass from him. He opted for a different approach to the previous games against a strong Chelsea side managed by Antonio Conté with their 5–2–3 formation that Bournemouth had not had any joy with before. Eddie also went for five at the back, but without their first-choice right-back, Adam Smith, Eddie put Ryan Fraser in as a wing-back in what he acknowledged was 'a slight risk' with a front three of Wilson, Stanislas and Ibe. Eddie set them up aggressively, with the front three pressing Chelsea's defenders and Fraser looking to burst forward, while their defenders had to work as a unit to nullify the threat of Chelsea's technically gifted midfielders like Eden Hazard. It was Bournemouth who broke the deadlock in the 51st minute, Wilson exchanging passes with Ibe, who put Wilson through to slot past Courtois. Seven minutes later, Wilson turned provider with a defence-splitting pass to Stanislas, who toe-poked it through Courtois' legs. Going 2–0 up at Stamford Bridge in the second half might have made other teams sit back and defend their lead, but Eddie had set them up to be confident and courageous, pushing for another if they got the chance. And three minutes later, Nathan Aké used terrific presence of mind to peel away from his marker and stay onside to divert in a shot from Stanislas. Eddie said to the BBC afterwards: 'We were very aggressive and everyone was magnificent. Our aggressiveness, work rate and endeavour – it all came together.' It was especially satisfying given that they'd been dumped out of the FA Cup quarter-final a few weeks earlier by Chelsea after an injury-time goal cancelled out Bournemouth's 90th-minute equaliser. That win, at the end of January, crowned a massive month for the club, winning two and drawing two, which sent them into the top half and also earned Eddie his second Manager of the Month award. Bournemouth finished the season in 12th, a solid mid-table performance, although Eddie, always ambitious to build and develop each season, would have no doubt seen this as a disappointing result.

It was another quiet summer, with Eddie only opting to bring in 21-year-old Welsh international attacking midfielder David Brooks from Sheffield United for £11.5 million, Diego Rico from Spanish club Leganés and Jefferson Lerma from Levante, both for undisclosed fees. The big buy was in the January transfer window, with 21-year-old striker Dominic Solanke joining Bournemouth from Liverpool for around £19 million, but his first season wouldn't be a great one, racking up just four goals.

The season had started brightly, with six wins in their first 10 games. Wilson had scored six and assisted four in his past 11 games and Bournemouth were sitting sixth in the table only a point away from Spurs, Arsenal and Chelsea. But form deserted them from November and continued until the new year, losing eight of their next 10 games. Back-to-back wins in January – the second of which was a morale-boosting 4–0 demolition of Chelsea – sent them back up to 10th, but they slid further down the table until a resounding 5–0 away win at Brighton in the middle of April effectively secured their Premier League status for another year. They finished in 14th, with a promising cup run again ended by Chelsea in the quarter-final, this time in the Carabao Cup, with Eden Hazard proving the difference between the two sides. It had been a bruising season for the Cherries, not helped by Callum Wilson suffering a hamstring injury and then a knee injury that took him out for 11 games. Still, even with those absences and recovery time, he managed 15 goals across all competitions, which is a strong return.

The following season, 2019–20, started fairly brightly with three wins in the first six games, but they'd only manage another six league wins all season. A late rally of two wins in four games, including a final day 3–1 away win at Goodison Park, was too little too late. They had to win that final game but they also needed Aston Villa and Watford to lose, which didn't happen. Thirty-four points was only enough for 18th place and their five-year campaign in the Premier League was at an end. It all took place in unsettling circumstances, with Covid-19 lockdowns forcing games to be played without fans present from March to the end of the season. Eddie was interviewed by BBC Radio 5 Live after the game, a lonely-looking figure on an eerily deserted Goodison Park pitch:

'Collectively, we haven't been good enough. I always think the league table, it's a cliché, but it doesn't lie, it tells a story and we've dipped below the levels that we were at in previous seasons, there's no denying that. As manager, I have to take the ultimate responsibility for that … We were great for the Premier League, the way such a small club can hold its own. We've been an inspiration for a lot of smaller clubs and it is so disappointing it has ended like this.'

On 1 August, Eddie left AFC Bournemouth by mutual consent, a decision that was said to have shocked players, staff and supporters. Incredibly, he was the longest-serving manager in the

Premier League at that point, having spent five seasons in the top division. He was Bournemouth's most successful manager – the man who had brought the club three promotions in six years. It brought to a close a relationship with the club spanning 25 years. In Eddie's emotional open letter to supporters, he said:

'I feel blessed to be able to leave the club with memories that will last a lifetime. Survival in 2009 followed by promotions in 2010, 2013 and 2015, leading to five fantastic years in the Premier League, are of course some of the major highlights, but I am most proud of the culture of the club that everyone involved in AFC Bournemouth has helped to build and create during that time. It is that culture that ultimately enabled us to enjoy the success that we did.'

He left Bournemouth a completely different club to the one he'd taken on as a 30-year-old manager. He'd established a culture of creative, entertaining and attacking football and he refused to change that style whomever they were playing against and whichever league they were in. Eddie acknowledged that they were always going to let in goals but they planned to score more than they'd concede. And for many seasons, it worked at Bournemouth, delighting Bournemouth fans and winning him many admirers. But it wasn't just the manager they'd miss at the club. They would miss the man that touched so many of their lives. The man who was famously pictured in an emotional embrace with Bournemouth midfielder Harry Arter, who had suffered a family tragedy just two days before insisting he was available for the match against Man United in December 2015 to take his mind off things at home. His players loved him not only for his tactical brilliance and commitment to bring out the best in each of them, but also for the man behind the manager. Local and national press were talking of Eddie's departure with terms like 'grief' and 'mourning'.

These were also terms that Eddie himself used to describe the immediate aftermath of leaving AFC Bournemouth. It was an emotional adjustment period followed by a few months of introspection, during which time he processed and analysed his career at the club and deconstructed what happened in his final season. He wanted to assess his strengths and weaknesses and get to the bottom of how he felt he had failed. It had been the first time in a relentless 12-year career in management to that point that he was able to pause and take stock.

He did have a loose plan in place, as he discussed with me in June 2023, saying: 'I'd sort of identified a year break. I wanted a minimum of 12 months to re-energise myself and get away from football for a little bit.' And at the end of it, he'd decide whether he wanted to get back into football management. He spent more time with his family, even buying a campervan so that he could travel around the UK with his boys. And he enjoyed the simple things that hadn't been previously possible due to the demanding nature of football management. He went to parents' evenings, took his children to school, took them to their school cricket matches and played football with them in the garden, but even then he couldn't help himself slipping back into coaching mode. He found it difficult to detach himself from football, but that was because he realised that it was part of his identity.

In November 2020, he took up one of the many offers to do sports media work, appearing on Sky Sports *Monday Night Football* alongside David Jones and Jamie Carragher. He answered questions about leaving Bournemouth and what he felt went wrong in that final season and reiterated that he'd made the best decision in the interests of both the club and himself going forward. He talked about finding it 'emotionally so difficult' in those first few weeks, and that's not surprising. The day you hang up your boots or leave your job on the staff at a football club, you're no longer connected to that everyday routine, the sense of collective enterprise, that intense but addictive environment. Suddenly you find yourself in a room by yourself. It's a massive change and takes a serious period of adjustment to adapt to it.

In the new-found time he had, he started listening to inspirational podcasts and reading books written by eminent people in sports. He started spending more and more time in his study, writing everything down that he'd learned in management – his training sessions, footballing philosophy, strategy and tactics, the culture he'd brought about – and categorised it all so he'd have a permanent resource to work from in the future. A managerial bible of sorts. It's something that he now uses every single day.

He built on the work that he started in 2015 to observe various different sporting clubs in order to broaden his knowledge. He visited eight, including Liverpool, and La Liga clubs Atlético Madrid and Rayo Vallecano, travelled to Denmark, spent time with the England national team, as well as rugby union club Saracens, paying particular attention to the culture of the club and how it contributed to their success. He also visited Shane McGuigan's boxing club and boxing promoter and former Leyton Orient owner Barry Hearn. He spoke to many former managers and businesspeople in football – CEOs and club owners – to give him an idea of what they valued in a manager, learning how much the personality of the manager influenced them.

Eddie picked up the next part of his story in our chat in June 2023: 'So as I was coming towards the end of that 12 months, I was like, right – what does that job look like that I would go back in for? It wasn't clear – I didn't have a row of clubs that I was looking at and going *that one, that one, that one*. I was sort of relying on my gut feeling to go when something cropped up that really, really took me.'

The first club to turn his head was Celtic in March 2021, after manager Neil Lennon left the club in February, 18 points adrift of Rangers in the table. Contrary to press reports that Eddie had performed a U-turn, pulling out of negotiations at the last minute, he was actually unable to assemble his backroom team, and he felt like they were the key to giving him the stability a pressurised job like that would have required. He wanted to be sure everything was right and in place before he committed to such an undertaking.

And then, in October 2021, word reached Eddie Howe that another club was looking for a new manager. This is what Eddie told me in June 2023 about that moment in time:

'The minute Newcastle United was mentioned, I knew instantly *that's the one*.'

CHAPTER 8

A **NEW** DAWN

Eddie Howe has got a wonderful calmness about him. He's very easy to like. When I asked him if he minded having a chat to me for this book, he didn't hesitate. One of the first things I asked him (June 2023) was what was it about Newcastle United that made him say to himself: 'This is the one.' This is what he told me:

'I think it was a combination of so many different things. It's the history of the club, the size of the club, the passion of the city – everything seemed to fit together really nicely. The coincidence was the takeover. For me, that wasn't really part of my thinking. But the optimism and the positivity that spread through the place from that moment made it even more desirable. I knew instantly that it was the one, but then it was a case of would they want me? And that you never quite know!'

What has always struck me about Eddie is his honesty, humility and warmth in conversation and the respect he has for whoever it is that's talking to him. He's calm, measured and focused. And as any TV/radio presenter, journalist or player he's managed will tell you, his attention to detail, preparation and work ethic is nothing short of extraordinary. When the right job came along, here at Newcastle United, he knew he might face an uphill battle. Not only was he likely to go up against some big-name managers, he'd also have to face down the stigma of taking a year out of the game. Gaps in the CV tend to be perceived to be a weakness, whatever business you're in, and he knew he'd have to confront that head-on. All he could do was present himself honestly and openly and rely on his experience, passion and vision to do the talking.

Eddie told me that after the club approached him, he was invited for an interview via Zoom, given the slow transition to normality after Covid restrictions had been lifted. Eddie found himself sitting in front of his computer at home presenting his vision for the club, footballing philosophy and ethos to Amanda Staveley, Mehrdad Ghodoussi, Jamie Reuben, chairman Yasir Al-Rumayyan and the other attendees. Many people would have found that a daunting and unsettling experience, not being there in person where you can project your personality so much better. But Eddie had forged a career in football management overcoming logistical difficulties and restrictions. He prepared for that meeting with a forensic attention to detail. He chose not to use any digital component to his presentation and he didn't use any notes – he felt that was the best way he could convey who he was and what he believed. That's just who Eddie is.

In that interview, Eddie highlighted how passionately he felt about training and developing players and how he felt it was his key strength. He also went into some depth about the squad he would be in charge of if he got the job. He'd put in a remarkable amount of research about every single squad member. He knew all of their strengths and the areas that he felt they could improve both individually and as a collective. He was already explaining what he'd do with the club in the January transfer window. Then he answered questions from the board members about him as a person and what he felt would make him a good fit at the club and with supporters.

Here's what Jamie Reuben, one of the club's directors, said about Eddie's interview to the Business of Sport podcast: 'What stood out ... which captivated the entire board, was just how prepared he was ... he talked specifically, whereas everybody else talked more generally, and for where we were in the league, it really resonated with us. He used specific players' names and he was so well rehearsed, he came with such a level of knowledge and we immediately felt very comfortable with him.'

But even with that spectacular showing in the interview, it was on a knife-edge between Eddie and Emery.

When Unai Emery was ultimately approached about the job on 3 November 2021, in a decision that split the five voting board members, Eddie didn't let it faze him. As he said in his first press conference at the club, those decisions were 'out of his hands. I just let the process happen.' He chose instead to focus on matters he could control. On the High Performance podcast in 2020, he spoke of the Emery situation with his trademark empathy and modesty. 'I understood if there was someone else that they wanted ahead of me, and someone with Unai's track record and how he's managed in Europe and the job he's done at other clubs – I probably would make the same decision if I was them, so I had no issues with it at all.'

After Emery chose to stay at Villarreal, Eddie was offered the job and agreed a two-and-a-half-year deal in principle. On 6 November, Eddie was seen sitting next to co-owners Amanda Staveley and Mehrdad Ghodoussi at the Amex Stadium watching Newcastle United fight back for a 1–1 draw with high-flying Brighton. Eddie hadn't even been confirmed yet as our new manager, but it felt like he was already having an impact on the players.

The club officially announced Eddie's appointment on 9 November, with Amanda Staveley stating: 'We have been incredibly impressed by Eddie through what has been a rigorous recruitment process. As well as his obvious achievements with AFC Bournemouth, where he had a transformational impact, he is a passionate and dynamic coach who has clear ideas about taking this team and club forward. He is a great fit for what we are trying to build here.'

In Eddie's first press conference on 10 November, he said, 'It feels fantastic to be head coach of Newcastle. I'm absolutely honoured, privileged, it's an incredible moment in my life and judging by the reaction I've had and how the two days of training has gone, it's been a really positive start.' His aim and that of the owners was crystal clear – do whatever it takes to stay in the Premier League.

A day or two later, Eddie made a decision that spoke volumes about him. He phoned up two club legends to ask them for their advice: Kevin Keegan and Alan Shearer. I was fortunate enough in June 2023 to talk to all three of them about what was said. First, here's Eddie:

'Respecting the history of the football club is hugely important. So when you go into somewhere new, you're very much having to prove yourself to everyone connected to the club. You can go one of two ways: you can go in and say *right, I'm going to do it totally my way, ignore all the noise and ignore everybody* – and there's nothing wrong with that approach – but what I wanted was to touch base with the history, and get an understanding of the club and of what had happened previously, both to help me and arm me with knowledge. So I spoke to Kevin, and it was really important that I did to get his experience and view on things and then Alan Shearer the same. I'm a believer in trying to connect the past to the present, so since that moment, there are a lot of former players that we've had in that I'd spoken to on the phone and connected with. That's just how I believe it should be done. There's no right or wrong but I think it's important with such a historic club, and there have been so many heroes over the years – so why not bring them closer to the club again.'

Here's what Kevin told me about the call from Eddie:

'I actually had a feeling he might ring me. I was on the road somewhere, driving with Jean, so I just pulled over to one side. It wasn't a long chat, it didn't need to be. I said, "Good luck, it's a great club, there's none like it in the world." Eddie asked for my advice and I said, "Just be honest with the people. Tell them what you can when you can." I got the feeling, which I said to Jean afterwards, that the club's in good hands here. They've got a guy who cares.

'Most of the other managers, they wouldn't ring me – I don't think any of them ever did to be honest with you. I guess Eddie wanted a bit of a steer. I had an advantage – my dad being a Geordie was a massive help for me. I knew the club and played there a lot. Eddie didn't have that benefit. He doesn't think he knows it all, and if he needs to ask questions, he's going to ask them and I'm delighted that he does. So many other managers in recent times, they don't get it. But he gets it and you've got to get that club.'

Alan Shearer echoed Kevin's sentiments in his phone call with Eddie, as he told me:

'I just said try and be as honest as possible with the fans, especially if you don't get results. Don't bulls**t them, and I understand you can't tell them everything but just be upfront with them because they'll really appreciate that. Like most football fans, we are hard-working people and if you give us the respect, and let us know how hard you're working and trying, they will absolutely love you – they'll adore you. I told him we just wanted a club that he would support with pride and he said he'd do his very best.'

Amusingly, Eddie actually moved into Alan Shearer's old house after he relocated to Newcastle, only Eddie had no idea it belonged to Alan, and Alan had no idea Eddie had moved into it. Eddie turned the telly on and saw a Netflix account named 'Al', but thought nothing of it, only that some bloke called Al used to live there!

I asked Eddie about what he felt like his welcome was in the city, and what the build-up was like to his first game in charge, against Brentford on 20 November 2021, and he told me:

'I knew that I had to be myself so you hope people like who you are, but I knew I wasn't going to be any different to how I've always been. I believe in telling it how it is, so if it's good or bad, tell the truth. I was welcomed into the training ground immediately. I felt like the people at the training ground who had been there for 10, 15, 25 years – there are some really loyal people in that training ground – they were very, very good with us. And I just hoped that people could see what we were trying to do with the team. We were trying to put our stamp on it and get the team to reflect the work that was going on at the time at the training ground. It's a very honest, hard-working team. I wanted our performances to reflect how important it was to play for Newcastle United. And thankfully, very early on, the response we were getting from the supporters was very positive. And I think that helped connect us all together and give the players more confidence when they entered the pitch.'

It helped that Eddie had three allies in the dressing room from the start – Callum Wilson, Matt Ritchie and Ryan Fraser – all of whom helped propel Bournemouth to the Premier League in 2015 under Eddie. But it's not enough just to have players in the dressing room who had played under you before – in Wilson, Ritchie and Fraser, he had three guys who respected him massively as a manager and trainer. It also meant they talked to the other guys in the Newcastle dressing room about what the squad could expect from Eddie: on the training front, it was going to be demanding and players would need to be switched on. And as a person, I'm sure they conveyed that Eddie was a fantastic man manager, honest and utterly committed to getting the best out of each of them. Eddie came into the dressing room with a vision of how we'd stay in the Premier League. And that vision drove his decision-making in a different way to that of a club sitting comfortably in mid-table or competing for the Champions League. He had to prioritise short-term survival over long-term ambition. And for that to work, he needed his players to fight for him. He needed to win their trust.

When Eddie joined the club, he held one-to-one meetings with every member of his squad, finding out about the person, not just the player. He wanted to understand how they worked, what drove them, learn about their upbringing and family life and how they came to be at Newcastle United. Then he set about working out a plan for how he could help each one. And to enter into that, there must be a huge bond of trust and mutual respect between them. I'm sure Eddie would have conveyed how committed he would be to bringing out the best in his players, but he needed that commitment and dedication back from each of them. To manage all of that, among 25 squad members, is quite an undertaking. You have to have extraordinary attention to detail, natural empathy, and an assistant manager and back-room team who are absolutely on the same page as you. You also have to genuinely care about your players. You get all of that right, and these guys are going to fight for you.

It wasn't just about development on the training pitch for Eddie. It was also about generating team spirit. He wanted his squad to bond properly as a group and show empathy and understanding towards each other. So when he took over, he went about this by encouraging a different player to share his personal story before their fortnightly meetings about player fines (for various infractions, like arriving late to training, not wearing the right kit etc.). As their leader, Eddie shared his personal story to the group in one of the first meetings, and told the High Performance podcast he found it 'quite emotional'. Everyone is silent during the talk to respect the speaker. Eddie created a comfortable and mutually supportive environment where there's no fear of judgement. Everyone could express themselves freely and I can see how that would bring a group closer together. It also has hugely positive long-term effects. Players will likely carry what they've learned and build on it to support each other when one of them might be struggling on the pitch or at home.

Here's what Ryan Fraser said about the effect of these meetings to NUFC TV:

'You respect each other more when you know certain things you didn't before. It means you go out and fight for each other.' And that's exactly what you need when you're expecting a relegation battle.

One of the first ideas Eddie came up with was to create a separate room next to the players' dressing room that was specifically for team talks. This sounds like it was partly to ensure focus from the players, where all they've got to concentrate on is the talk at hand. In a usual dressing-room environment, players are adjusting boots and other bits of kit and there can be a lot of noise, but Eddie's solution ensured calm and concentration. It was also designed so that their dressing room became their own private space as a group. He was doing everything he could to improve team spirit and confidence.

Eddie found from very early on that almost all of his squad responded very well to his training methods and his commitment to helping each one of them achieve their potential, which is no mean feat when you're dealing with players with all different levels of experience, personalities and goals of their own. Eddie focuses on his players' strengths and uses that as a platform from which to improve other areas about their game. Focusing on the positives comes naturally to Eddie when he's dealing with other people; it's a different matter when he's talking about himself, where he tends to focus on the negatives. The person he's hardest on is himself, but I think that's part and parcel of a high-achiever with obsessive attention to detail and an inbuilt drive to succeed. He's always thinking of what could be bettered, as former Bournemouth striker Yann Kermorgant told Chronicle Live in November 2021: 'As soon as we finished the game, Eddie was already on the computer watching it and trying to find why we had not been better than we were.'

. . .

Eddie was working tirelessly in the build-up to his first game in charge at Newcastle United, but we had a mountain to climb. We were 19th in the table and five points from safety. And frustratingly, Eddie didn't get to direct proceedings from the dugout at St James' Park for his first match, against Brentford, because he'd come down with Covid, so he watched it in his hotel room. Not ideal.

Even though he wasn't there in person, on the pitch the performance was instantly miles better than before and the whole vibe of the club was pulsing. You could see that the players were working harder on the pitch. They had the hunger to chase down that ball, press the opposition and keep it going until full-time. We came from behind twice to draw 3–3 and it was one of those games that we probably would have lost before he joined. Eddie had given us some fight again.

While Eddie's impact didn't translate to wins at first, everyone in the ground had the sense that things were gradually going in the right direction. In the next match, against Arsenal, we put in a decent performance. Yes, we lost 2–0 but we racked up five shots on target. Still, we desperately needed to get some points on the board because the numbers didn't make for great reading. We were bottom of the table, had played 13 games and were on six points, seven adrift of 16th-placed Watford. The next match, against 19th-placed Norwich, on 30 November 2021, was already looking like a must-win match. But we had a shocker in the first 10 minutes, with Ciaran Clark sent off for pulling back Teemu Pukki as he advanced on goal. It was the last thing we needed. But that moment proved to be a career-changing moment for Joelinton. Eddie had an idea and told him to play in central midfield for the rest of the game.

To give a bit of background to that moment, Joelinton hadn't been achieving anything like his potential at Newcastle United as a centre-forward. He had joined Brazilian club Recife's youth team in 2010, aged 14, and made his professional debut in 2014, the season they'd been promoted into Brazil's Série A. He scored five times the following season but was sent off in two successive games. He was signed by German club 1899 Hoffenheim in June 2015 on a five-year deal, only playing one game before being loaned out in summer 2016 to Austrian club Rapid Vienna, where he impressed, scoring 15 goals in 60 games, including an injury-time winner that sent them into the Austrian Cup final in 2017.

When he returned to 1899 Hoffenheim for the 2018–19 season, he made 27 appearances, scoring his first goal in the Bundesliga, a hat-trick in the DFB-Pokal (German domestic cup) and his first Champions League goal. That all attracted the attention of big clubs in Europe, but it was Newcastle United that got the young striker, who signed a six-year deal in July 2019 for a reported £40 million and picked up the coveted number 9 shirt. He scored his first goal (the winner) against Spurs away on 25 August 2019 and then didn't hit the back of the net again until January, against League One Rochdale in the FA Cup. He scored four times that season in 44 appearances. The next season wasn't much of an improvement, with six goals in 36 games. He was being talked about by fans as one of the club's worst signings.

But in that match against Norwich in 2021 playing as a midfielder for the first time at Newcastle United, he defended solidly, threw himself into challenges, closed down whoever was on the ball and seemed to have limitless energy. We would have held on for the win were it not for Pukki's spectacular volley late on in the game. Joelinton admitted to being nervous about what Eddie asked him to do, especially because in the last game he played as a number 8, at Rapid Vienna, he got sent off in the local derby and they lost. That kind of memory would haunt you. But for us, he had an absolute blinder. Here's what Eddie said a couple of days after the game:

'He covered every blade of grass the other night and put in tackles you wouldn't associate with a centre-forward. The tactical delivery of what we asked him to do, in two different positions, was of the highest level.'

At the end of November, we had become only the fourth team in Premier League history to go winless for 14 games. But it wouldn't get to 15.

We recorded our first win of the season in Eddie's fourth game in charge, at home against Burnley in early December. I remember celebrating with my son Will when Callum Wilson snatched the ball from Burnley keeper Nick Pope before side-stepping to the right and finding a way past three Burnley players and shooting into the roof of the net. We were the ones pressing for a second towards the end of the game and you could see how much it meant to Eddie, pumping his fists at the final whistle.

It felt like a launch pad but difficult games followed against Leicester and Liverpool away before Man City at home, all of which we lost, shipping 11 goals and only scoring once. But we found a way to bounce back with a 1–1 draw with Man United on 27 December, which really should have been a win were it not for David de Gea somehow keeping out Miguel Almirón's follow-up after Jacob Murphy hit the post towards the final whistle. We were showing signs of recovery. Joelinton in particular was incredible, creating the most chances, making the most interceptions, winning possession the most times, topping almost every stat category. He was the best player on the night and was a fully deserved recipient of the Man of the Match award. You could see and hear how thrilled Sean Longstaff was for him in an interview they did together with Sky Sports after the match. 'He's shown since the manager came in what he's been like in training. Everyone at the club rates him so highly. The noise from outside is so disrespectful and if you watch him enough you see how good he is. I'm so happy for him and proud of him.'

This was such an unusual response from a footballer to an interview question, to answer with such emotional honesty. You have to be in a truly mutually supportive environment to be able to say that, and that's testament to the culture Eddie has spearheaded at the club.

Rather than cast Joelinton aside, as so many coaches might have done, Eddie Howe had seen an opportunity, identified the raw talent that Joelinton had and found a way to harness it in a way that benefitted the player and the team. Eddie would have invested much time and energy into a dedicated training regime just for Joelinton, the extra attention no doubt giving him self-belief and confidence. And that has not only fed into the whole team, but on to the terraces as well.

A hugely exciting development was taking place behind the scenes during that time as well, in late December 2021, with the breaking news that Brighton and Hove Albion's technical director, Dan Ashworth, had been granted permission by the club to talk to Newcastle United. Dan Ashworth is a former player turned sporting director and is a big deal in football circles. He was the Football Association's technical director between 2012 and 2018 and a massive reason behind the transformation of the organisation, pioneering the 'England DNA' development plan to create winning senior teams in both the men's and women's game. His impact was summed up by England manager Gareth Southgate, when Ashworth left the FA to join Brighton as technical director, shortly after Dan and Gareth attended the annual FIFA and UEFA technical conferences in September 2018:

'The last time we came to one of these it was in St Petersburg three years ago, but this time we walked in as world champions at U-17 and U-20 and we've been to a seniors' semi-final, so we deserve our place at the table. That is a great credit to everyone involved, the backing the FA has given us in building St George's Park and investing in the teams, to the work being done in youth development and to Dan in particular for putting those plans in place, which we have seen pay off for Spain, Germany and France.'

One of Dan Ashworth's key accomplishments at Brighton was building a young squad for the future. This isn't a guy who was buying players young and selling them off for a profit, as we'd seen under Mike Ashley's ownership. He wanted to sign young players, help them achieve their potential, often by loaning them out to good clubs abroad before they'd be at Brighton for their prime years. He had a long-term ambition for the club, so you can see why these qualities chimed with Amanda, Mehrdad and Jamie. Bringing Dan Ashworth to St James' Park, which finally happened in summer 2022, was a major coup for Newcastle United. In June 2023, Kevin Keegan summed up to me why Ashworth joining Newcastle said a lot about the new owners:

'What I see at Newcastle is people owning it who've got money, who know that they don't know that much about football, but are employing people and finding people who do know. With player recruitment under Dan Ashworth, I'm confident that it's going to work because they're not just coming in and saying to the manager, "What do you want? Here you go." They're actually putting scaffolding around him and helping him to build. That's what makes me confident that it's for the long term.'

On the pitch in the new year, it all starting gelling together. The massive turning point was Leeds away. I was at Elland Road with Will, and we were scrapping for points at that stage, because relegation was still very much a factor. The atmosphere at Elland Road in the away end was feverish – everyone singing, chanting, biting fingernails – we experienced it all together. Will looked at me and said, 'Dad – this is a bit mental!' with a smile on his face. I knew how he felt. I felt it when I was a lad. In that Leeds game, Jonjo Shelvey scored the winner with a well-struck low free kick in the 75th minute and the whole away stand felt like it was shaking. But we were sick with nerves after that, trying to close out the win. Joe Willock very nearly scored in stoppage time, which would have given my heart a rest, but the final whistle went and we'd earned a very-hard-fought second win of the season. It felt like a seismic result and just rewards for the work going on at the club.

That period coincided with Eddie's first transfer window at the club. He had a clear aim with his first transfer deal, which proved to be a landmark signing for him: England international Kieron Trippier, who'd played for Eddie when he was manager of Burnley. In the High Performance podcast in November 2022, Eddie explained his thought process at that time: 'When we signed Kieron in January, we were trying to sign leaders ... We felt that we couldn't sign players for the future; it was for the here and now and it was trying to generate a team spirit in the group that will be so strong that it will carry us over the line.'

Trippier was such a big signing, because it signalled that we were able to attract that next level of player. And it felt like it helped him make some incredible signings later that month – Brazilian international Bruno Guimarães, Dan Burn and Matt Targett (on loan) – and they'll be forever loved by Newcastle United fans for that because they all took a serious risk. Bruno proved to be a phenomenally talented game-changer of a signing. We also signed striker Chris Wood from Burnley during that transfer window, and although he didn't score that many goals for us, he did score a couple of useful ones while Callum Wilson was out injured. Plus, buying him weakened Burnley, who at that point looked like they'd be with us in the relegation dogfight. It seemed like a shrewd tactical purchase.

The next game, on 8 February 2022, was, in the end, a convincing and morale-boosting win against Everton at St James' Park. It wasn't looking so great after seeing the ball cannon off Jamaal Lascelles and into our net after 36 minutes, but Lascelles didn't let it get to him, and barely two minutes later he powered a Trippier corner against the crossbar and back off Mason Holgate into the net. The second Newcastle goal wasn't pretty, with Ryan Fraser bundling it in after Allan Saint-Maximin sprinted to the byline and sent over an inviting cross. And then Trippier made sure the vital points would be staying with us after a fantastic free kick from 30 yards out curled into the bottom corner. It could have been four when Saint-Maximin found Jacob Murphy but his effort from just inside the box hit the post.

That win was a big psychological boost, securing back-to-back victories. More importantly, it lifted us out of the drop zone. And it got better after Villa came to town five days later. Trippier was the difference once more, scoring his second free kick in two games. Yes, a deflection wrong-footed Argentinian number-one keeper Emiliano Martínez, but it was hit with such power that he was powerless to stop it passing him. An Ollie Watkins header early on in the second half was thankfully ruled out for a marginal offside on VAR, which was celebrated by the home fans like a goal. The relief was palpable when the final whistle blew. Three wins in three and we were climbing that table. Plus, we were getting stronger on the field, Eddie Howe's tactics were running through the veins of the players and the noise levels were well and truly back at St James' Park.

Everyone started to buy into what Eddie was selling. We'd had one promising-looking false start after beating Burnley in December, but this time, we were kicking on.

Next up was a tough one against Champions League-chasing West Ham at the London Stadium and we played out a hard-fought 1–1 draw, Joe Willock equalising on the verge of half-time in a game that petered out in the second half. The next match, away at Brentford, on 26 February, was an emotional one. Christian Eriksen, who'd suffered a cardiac arrest on the field at Euro 2020 in Denmark's match against Finland, was back on a football field, 259 days later. Everyone in the stadium rose to their feet in the 52nd minute when he came on as a substitute. But the game was almost over by that point – Josh Dasilva was sent off for Brentford after just 11 minutes for a dangerous tackle and we were 2–0 up at half-time, Joelinton rising high and arrowing a powerful header into the corner for the first goal. He reacted by instinctively sprinting to the away stand, roaring, with his arms outstretched. You could tell what a huge moment it was for him. It reminded me of that moment in *The Shawshank Redemption* when Andy Dufresne broke free, after navigating a sewage pipe full of sh*t. Joelinton had completely reinvented himself as a powerful box-to-box midfielder and was being compared by pundits and the press to Patrick Vieira and Yaya Touré.

Eddie had given him the tools to redeem himself – the rest he did through sheer hard work and courage. A couple of months later, he was voted the club's official Player of the Year. It was a sensational turnaround and no less than his effort and commitment deserved. A new chant started at the Gallowgate End in Joelinton's honour, to the tune of 'She's Electric':

'He's Brazilian. He only cost £40 million. We think he's f*****g brilliant. It's Joe-lin-ton.'

That emotionally charged match against Brentford marked the end of February 2022 – a hugely successful month, with three wins and a draw in four games. It earned Eddie Howe his first Manager of the Month accolade as boss of the Magpies. It was an incredible achievement after only three months in charge. Here's what he said after receiving the award:

'A lot of questions were asked of our resilience and resolve, and ability to bounce back from what seemed, at some stages, I wouldn't say impossible, but a very difficult moment, and that's where the players have really stepped up … They deserve a lot of credit for how they've attacked this spell of games and confidence has returned with every win.'

Eddie had set up the team to start games at a very high tempo, which unsettled the opposition, and that's exactly what happened in the next game against Brighton, with Ryan Fraser keeping up with Joe Willock's run to be in the right place at the right time to turn in the rebound off the post after 12 minutes. And two minutes later, Fraser was at it again, this time sending in an inch-perfect cross that Fabian Schär met with a powerful header. Brighton came back into the game strongly, dominating possession and finding a way back in with a Lewis Dunk header from a corner. That triggered a very nervous half-hour at St James' Park, but we held firm and ground out the win.

Bruno turned in a man-of-the-match-winning performance in the following game against Southampton away, scoring his first goal for the club with an absolutely ridiculous volleyed back-heel in front of the travelling Geordie fans, which proved to be the winner. It was actually like watching Brazil. The away end erupted and I remember people falling over the rows either side of me. Bruno was fast becoming a cult hero on the terraces and the loud chants of 'BRUNO, BRUNO' continued long after the final whistle. Fears of relegation had slipped away and it was starting to feel like a case of how high up the table we could finish. We'd won three in a row again and were unbeaten in nine games.

The next game we got pretty unlucky with. At Stamford Bridge facing Champions League-holders Chelsea, Almirón was unfortunate to see his stunning volley from the edge of the box parried by Édouard Mendy before Bruno went close with a drive that zipped past the far post. And we really should have had a penalty in the second half when Trevoh Chalobah was all over Jacob Murphy. But when things aren't going your way, sometimes there's not much you can do about it, and in the 89th minute, Dan Burn slipped, allowing Kai Havertz to break free, neatly control the ball in the box and fire past Martin Dúbravka. It brought an end to our unbeaten run in slightly cruel fashion.

Luck really wasn't on our side in the next game either. We had plenty of chances and a lot of ball against Everton at Goodison Park but it was a pretty scrappy game. After a protester tied himself to one of the posts in the second half, there was an eight-minute delay. Everton went down to 10 men after Allan's yellow card for a cynical foul on Saint-Maximin was upgraded to a red by VAR. We were pushing for a winner and went close through Willock but we were caught out by an interception by Seamus Coleman, who fed Alex Iwobi, who then exchanged passes with Dominic Calvert-Lewin before firing a heartbreaking left-foot shot past Dúbravka in the 99th minute. It was gutting. We'd had 17 shots and six on target in that game. Everton manager Frank Lampard celebrated so much he broke his hand.

A heavy 5–1 away loss to Champions League-chasing Spurs in London was a blip. We left ourselves massively exposed after going behind and trying to find an equaliser but just fell apart in the second half. But things weren't looking too bad when you looked at the table – we were nine points clear of relegation. Still, we needed a strong performance against eighth-placed Wolves to stop the rot. What we got was a gritty display, and that's what we needed. Chris Wood stepped up in that game when we needed him, first winning a penalty, then blasting it home at the Gallowgate End. Dúbravka had to be on his toes late on to deny what felt like Wolves' only shot on target in the game. And with that, we gratefully collected another three points.

We built on that determined display with three wins on the trot, coming from behind against Leicester to equalise through Bruno's persistence, finding a way to stab it through Kasper Schmeichel's legs when both players were on the floor. And then, in the 95th minute, after some fantastic work from Joe Willock, Bruno launched a diving header into the top corner and sent the Gallowgate into dreamland.

Bruno was at it again in the next game against Crystal Palace, on 20 April 2022, lofting a pass to set Almirón free down the right, who nodded it towards the penalty area, outmuscling and outpacing Tyrick Mitchell before powering a left-footed shot into the top corner. What a goal. A late rally from Palace wasn't enough and we saw the victory out. That took us to 40 points – the magic number that's almost always enough to avoid relegation* – and we still had five games left to play. It was an incredible turnaround and St James' was becoming a fortress – we'd won the past six home games and hadn't lost since the Chelsea match in October.

And it was another three points in the bag after a great away performance against Norwich, a neat bit of work in the box teeing up Joelinton who absolutely leathered it home off the crossbar. We were full of confidence and working amazingly as a team, none more so than when Jacob Murphy broke free and rather than taking the shot on, fooled everyone by unselfishly squaring it to Joelinton for a tap-in. What a way to mark your 100th Premier League game. Just after the break, Tim Krul passed the ball along the ground towards Kenny McLean but Bruno showed his hunger, stretching to intercept it, rolling the ball forward with his studs and then casually chipping the diving Krul. The 3–0 scoreline flattered Norwich if anything. We were rampant.

The atmosphere for our next home game, against Liverpool, was incredible. And to be fair, our form in 2022 would have

---

* Only Sunderland in 1997, Bolton in 1998 and West Ham in 2003 have gone down with 40 points or more at the end of the season.

put us in third place, behind Man City and Liverpool. And in Liverpool, we were facing a team still very much on for the quadruple – they'd already won the Carabao Cup, were in the final of the FA Cup after beating Man City in the semis, and had just recorded a 2–0 win in the first leg of the Champions League semi-final. They had to win to stay level with Man City in the league. Dúbravka had a blinding game, keeping out Jota numerous times. The only one he wasn't equal to, after Keita went round him, shouldn't have stood, coming after a clear foul on Schär by James Milner in the build-up. The boos around St James' were louder than the Liverpool cheers, but the truth is we were outclassed in that game by an excellent side.

We faced another excellent side just over a week later, at the Etihad. It was a straight shoot-out with Liverpool for the title and City had to win. And they came into the game all fired up after capitulating in that incredible Champions League semi-final second leg at the Bernabeu against Real Madrid. They were unstoppable against us that day. I'm not sure any team could have lived with them.

We needed to bounce back at home in the penultimate game of the season, against Arsenal. During that match, the excitement level really ramped up. It was packed to the rafters – Arsenal were desperate to overtake Spurs and make it to the Champions League place, and the atmosphere was off the scale. In the first minute, the ball got played back to Aaron Ramsdale and he tried to clear it but he sliced it horribly and they looked like they were sh*tting themselves. It felt like we battered them in the first half and we were expecting them to come back out and put us to the sword in the second half, but it just carried on like it did in the first half. Wilson's persistence forced an own goal from Ben White before Bruno rolled in a second with time ticking away. The noise levels when that goal went in were incredible. I remember fans from other teams criticising the Geordies for celebrating when they hadn't actually won anything. But the truth is we had. We'd won something better than a trophy. We'd won our football club back. After the full-time whistle, Eddie led the players on a lap of honour. Amanda Staveley was on the field, so were Ant and Dec. I worked my way down from the press box down to where my mum and dad always sit in the Milburn Stand. Mum was crying her eyes out and I could just about make out the sentence: 'It's not been like this since Bobby!' That was the moment that I thought *next season's going to be brilliant.*

For the final game of the season, me, my son Will, his mate and his dad all piled into the car for an away day to Burnley and it just felt like a party atmosphere, the whole day, everyone wearing bucket hats and Hawaiian shirts with Joelinton on them that had taken off in February 2022. There was no pressure on us – it was just a really enjoyable day out watching the team we love. It was the first time I'd taken my son to an away game. Until then, at away games, we wouldn't have that great a chance of winning, and it's a long way for a young lad only to watch your team lose, but at the back end of the 2021–22 season, I thought why not?! He bloody loved it. There's nothing like an away day when you win. And all Will's seen have been victories, so he's become a good-luck charm. When the fixtures list for 2024 came out recently, the first thing he said was, 'What away days are we doing, Dad?!'

Burnley needed to win to stay up, while we were happily mid-table with nothing to play for, but we still went there and won. Wilson was back from injury and scored twice, much to everyone's delight. The sun was shining, and everyone in black and white was singing and talking to each other about how excited they were for next season.

From the day he joined the club, Eddie went about his task – to keep us in the Premier League – with utter focus and single-minded determination. He very much viewed relegation in his final season at Bournemouth as a personal failure, seeing the manager as the captain of the ship who has to take ultimate responsibility for the direction they're travelling in. But the failure, as he sees it, didn't come about through a lack of application. So he went about improving himself in that time away from the game by broadening his mind, going out and seeing how things were done at other clubs, reading about new ideas and formulating his own. He's a man constantly seeking to evolve, and looking for ways to help others to do the same. The time that he'd taken out of the game had prepared him for this moment, to take charge at Newcastle United, and he hit the ground running. It demonstrated the hugely positive impact a period of time away, before stepping back, can do to help you in a high-pressured environment that demands so much of you practically 24/7.

In the 2021–22 season, Eddie Howe had turned us from relegation certainties into a solid mid-table club. On New Year's Day 2022, we were in 19th place, on 11 points. We were the draw specialists, with eight draws. In the second half of the season, we picked up 38 points and finished in 11th place. It was a remarkable transformation.

Meanwhile, behind the scenes, another transformation was about to take place, after a rigorous recruitment process to find a chief executive officer delivered one of the best in the business. We'd been without a CEO since Lee Charnley left the club in November 2021, and, once again, the new owners demonstrated that they would take the time and put in the legwork to find the perfect fit. Darren Eales was recruited from Major League Soccer (MLS) side Atlanta United FC, where he'd been president and chief executive from 2014 to 2022, joining the club in the year of their foundation. His achievements in that period had been astonishing, literally building the club up from nothing and masterminding their huge success, winning the MLS Eastern Conference and the MLS Cup, as well as securing the highest average attendance in the league only a year after Atlanta United FC joined the MLS in 2017. He was rewarded for his achievements by being named MLS Executive of the Year twice and was named Best Executive by the World Football Summit in 2019.

Darren had played football both in the UK and the US at university/college level as a striker, and was a seriously promising player, being awarded Ivy League Player of the Year in 1994 and becoming a first-team All American (one of the top 11 US college soccer players that year) the same year, before going on to play in the second division of US football. He ultimately chose a career in law over professional football, returning to England and training as a barrister. But he combined his skills, becoming a lawyer at West Bromwich Albion in 2006, rising up to director and company secretary. From 2006 to 2010 he worked with Dan Ashworth at the club, while West Brom re-established themselves in the Premier League. Eales was recruited by Spurs in 2010 as executive director and he was the man responsible for some stunning deals there, managing to sign Rafael van der Vaart after getting the nod from Daniel Levy just 90 minutes before the transfer window shut. He also recruited Hugo Lloris and manager Mauricio Pochettino as well as negotiating some amazing sales too, including Gareth Bale signing for Real Madrid for a world record £86 million.

The club announced the appointment of Eales on 15 July 2022 and here's what he had to say:

'Newcastle United is both a giant of a club and the heartbeat of its community. Every time I have visited St James' Park, I've been overwhelmed by the passion of the fans. This is a club with an amazingly rich heritage, and I am delighted to be joining for this new chapter in its long history.'

I'm not sure you get any more on the money than that. The club had hired an exceptional, proven winner. With Eddie and his backroom team driving performances on the pitch and the players responding magnificently to it, we'd weathered the storm in the short term and secured our survival. And with two hugely respected, influential executives joining the club at the top of their respective games, there was the sense that the owners were putting us in a position to compete in the long term. And the supporters had full faith that they knew what they were doing. Roll on next season!

CHAPTER 9

KICKING ON

I can't remember feeling as much excitement around Newcastle as I felt before the start of the 2022–23 season. One of the really noticeable changes was that people were suddenly buying shirts, scarves, flags and merchandise again. Now that the whole miserable Ashley saga was behind us, it was like the city had changed colour. Fans weren't worried about lining Ashley's pockets any more when they knew he wouldn't reinvest their hard-earned cash in the squad. Under the new management and ownership, we felt optimistic about the long-term future of the club. And that translated into queues of people in the club shop and lines of folks inside the ground buying pies and pints. Supporters were desperate to hand over their money again because it felt like we were helping to grow the club. It felt, finally, like we're all in this together again. In the ground itself, the whole place was a rippling sea of black and white. And the noise had started to rival the legendary 1992–93 season under Kevin Keegan.

Newspapers and sports websites were all predicting serious progress for Newcastle United's 2022–23 season. The *Guardian* reckoned we'd finish seventh as did *FourFourTwo*, while several 'supercomputers' in the tabloids were making hefty predictions, too. Suddenly, we were being linked with Mbappé, Neymar and

Messi, and while I knew those kinds of deals weren't going to happen, not least because of the financial fair play restrictions that had been introduced to ensure clubs weren't spending more than they earned, the fact that players of that quality were being talked about produced an air of pre-season optimism that most of the Toon Army hadn't felt in decades. The reality was, most fans would have been happy to settle for a season where fears of relegation weren't a constant threat. A nice cosy mid-table season where we could all relax and enjoy some occasional decent performances would have done for most of us. Not even the most optimistic Geordie would have predicted what was to come …

Eddie Howe made some big signings in the 2022 summer break: goalkeeper Nick Pope joined us from Burnley for £10 million and 22-year-old Dutch centre-back Sven Botman was recruited from Lille for £35 million, choosing Newcastle United over little-known Italian club AC Milan. These were the kinds of deals that made us feel like the club had a clear vision for building long-term success. Pope was an established and dependable keeper, who'd earned himself the number 1 spot in the PFA Team of the Year in 2019 and had won 10 caps for England since his international debut in 2018. Botman was simply one of the most promising centre-backs in Europe. He'd joined Lille in July 2020 before the 2020–21 season and the 20-year-old went straight into the starting eleven. That season, Lille won the French Ligue 1 title for the first time in 10 years, pipping perennial champions Paris Saint-Germain to the title. While PSG scored more goals than Lille, Lille conceded the fewest number of goals (23) in the league. It doesn't take a genius to conclude that their win was built from a rock-solid foundation at the back. And that was the key area that Eddie wanted to develop at Newcastle United.

An opening day fixture at home against newly promoted Nottingham Forest was the perfect way to start the 2022–23 season. It was a decent day – the sun broke through the clouds before kick-off and everyone was in such a good mood heading past the statues of Shearer and Sir Bobby and up into the Milburn Stand. Supporters were kitted out in the new kits, singing, drinking outside whilst drinking in the atmosphere. 'It's a new dawn, it's a new day, it's a new life for NUFC ... and we're feeling good,' read a massive banner moving along the Gallowgate End. Then the song itself blasted out around the ground. You can't beat the opening day of the season buzz, but this was a bigger buzz than I'd felt in years, possibly ever. Then you know it's nearly 3pm when 'Blaydon Races' and 'Hey Jude' ring out around the ground. It's all part of the Saturday service at the Cathedral on the Hill before the players run out to Mark Knopfler's anthemic 'Local Hero'. That euphoric guitar and saxophone combo never fails to lift you up and you soak in that special shared moment around family, friends and the community you belong to.

To be honest, the whole afternoon just felt really comfortable. New signing Nick Pope started in goal; it felt like we were in control from the first minute and we attacked from the off. It took until the 58th minute to find the breakthrough and the ground erupted when Fabian Schär's long-range effort flew into the top corner past Dean Henderson. In the end we ran out 2–0 winners but it should have been a lot more. Howe's team had fired in 23 shots, 10 of which were on target, while Forest didn't register a single shot on target. It was an unfamiliar sensation, feeling like the opposition just weren't going to score. It was a dominant display to kick off the season and the fans were buoyant as they spilled into the bars and clubs of Tyneside after the match.

The second game of the season was a scoreless draw at the Amex, which felt at the time like a bit of a disappointment, but given how good Brighton were all season, it was a decent result. The next game was a massive test, against Man City at home. For all the optimism swirling around St James' Park, it didn't escape my attention that in the two games the previous season against Man City, we'd lost, on aggregate, 9–0.

Before that massively testing match at home against Man City, supporters group Wor Flags brought out a banner that read 'Wor Miggy', featuring fan favourite Miguel Almirón waving a black-and-white banner. It was to show solidarity with Almirón after a weirdly disrespectful comment Jack Grealish made about him during Man City's Premier League title celebrations the previous summer. Although no one could doubt Almirón's effort and energy, he had come in for a lot of criticism for his lack of end product, both in terms of goals and assists. He had been signed by Rafa Benítez at the end of the January transfer window in 2019 from MLS team Atlanta United for £21 million, smashing the previous record of £16.5 million paid to Real Madrid for Michael Owen in 2005, and so expectations were high from the moment he stepped on to the pitch. It didn't help that just two months after making his debut, he went down with a serious hamstring injury after a tackle from Southampton's Oriol Romeu and was ruled out for the rest of the 2018–19 season. Almirón had been our top scorer in the 2019–20 season under Steve Bruce. He'd managed to score eight goals in all competitions (four in the Premier League and four in the FA Cup) in 42 matches. It was an OK season, but barely anything more. To be honest, the fact that return made him top scorer underlined how bad things were that season under Bruce. The future wasn't looking great for Almirón even after Eddie had taken charge in October 2021. Under Eddie Howe, Miggy had only scored once and provided no assists in 32 games. Rumours were swirling that he could be sold off in the summer at a loss just to raise some funds. Despite all that he was always a fairly popular figure with supporters and in truth he's the kind of lad that you're always just willing to do well. But then, the hard work that Almirón, Eddie, Jason Tindall and the coaching staff had been putting in during training and in the analysis room finally started to come together.

That Man City game was absolutely ridiculous. It was end to end from the whistle. After a breathless first five minutes, Bernardo Silva (far too easily) picked out Ilkay Gündogan in the box, who sent it past Nick Pope – the first goal he'd conceded so far that season. It could have followed a predictable pattern for Man City after that, but not this time. Eddie Howe's sides don't lie down and we rallied. Some great work from Allan Saint-Maximin down the left produced a dangerous cross which Miggy Almirón somehow turned home! There was a nervous wait as VAR looked at whether Miggy was onside and which part of his body the ball had come off. The atmosphere cranked up a notch when Callum Wilson thumped home our second goal with the outside of his foot after another probing run by Saint-Maximin on 39 minutes. When the half-time whistle blew we were leading the champions 2–1 and we'd shown immense character to come back from a goal down. Surely the second half was going to be explosive. City would come back firing. Half the stadium probably needed a lie down. Into the second half and the big question in everyone's mind was: *Can we do this? Can we beat the champions?* Nine minutes after the break it appeared the answer was a firm YES. Kieran Trippier stood over a free kick 30 yards out and the crowd fell silent in anticipation. He took three paces backwards, then stepped up with purpose and dispatched an unstoppable curling effort into the top corner past Ederson. An absolutely unbelievable strike and the whole of Tyneside plus Geordies watching around the world all completely lost their sh*t.

We were 3–1 up against the champions. *Is this actually happening?*, I had to keep asking myself. Of course, Haaland spoiled the party by bludgeoning the ball in and then De Bruyne did what he does, threading a wonder ball forward to Bernardo Silva and suddenly it's 3–3. But what a game. And we proved that we were a match for the best out there. Almirón had done his talking on the pitch and had a great game, prompting Eddie Howe to say afterwards to Sky Sports: 'I'm proud of Miggy. Near enough every time he puts a football shirt on, he's an incredible guy. I thought it was a lovely touch from the supporters again today; they're such an understanding group. They've shown their support for Miggy today, he's scored a goal – [I'm] really pleased for him.'

On paper we only had five points from our opening three games, but you look at what those games were: winning against a newly promoted team at home, drawing away to a really strong Brighton side and drawing at home against Man City, and it's a good start, by anyone's standards.

Then came some incredible news on 26 August 2022. Eddie had broken the club record to sign a player that had got everyone talking: Alexander Isak, the hugely exciting 22-year-old striker from Real Sociedad. The 6ft 4in forward had already racked up over 40 appearances for Sweden since his debut as a 17-year-old and had scored nine times. He already had a taste of silverware at Real Sociedad, helping them win the Copa del Rey in 2021. He was the top scorer in the tournament, including two fantastic goals in a memorable 4–3 win against Real Madrid at the Bernabeu that made every top European manager take notice. My old mate Keith Downie interviewed Eddie for Sky Sports two days after Isak signed and here's what Eddie said:

'I think he's an outstanding talent. He's got the right profile for us. He's young, there's definite scope to improve with us as we go through our journey here … he's technically very good, he's very quick, he's a versatile player as well, so I think he ticks all the boxes for us.'

He certainly fitted the mould that Eddie was looking for. And although he was reluctant to use the term, Isak was a statement signing.

We didn't get going in the next game, needing a last-minute Saint-Maximin goal to level things up against Wolves. Then came Liverpool at Anfield, and excited anticipation of Isak's debut. And wow, he totally lived up to his billing. He scored and put us 1–0 up in the first half with an emphatic finish, then scored another one in the second half, turning two Liverpool defenders in the process, but it was given as offside on VAR, which still to this day baffles me because they drew the two sets of lines on the screen like they do with VAR, but Liverpool defender Joe Gomez's foot looked like it was playing Isak onside. That would have been 2–0 and the game would have been completely different. As it was, Firmino equalised just after the hour mark and it looked as though it was going to end 1–1 until Liverpool midfielder Fábio Carvalho bundled in from a corner with virtually the last kick of the game (after 98 minutes, although the last kick of the game should have been about three minutes before then).

Liverpool made a lot of the fact we were trying to run down the clock, with their fans booing our players off the pitch and Klopp complaining about time-wasting in the post-match interviews, but it was later revealed that out of all the matches played so far in the Premier League that season, it was the ninth highest in terms of how long the ball was actually in play. Either way, we Newcastle United fans all left thinking we deserved to win that game and I remember saying to my mates at the time: 'We're better than Liverpool, you know.' Isak's outstanding performance on his debut won him the man of the match award. This guy was the real deal. But he went down injured two games later and we wouldn't see him back on the pitch until the new year.

We started October by thumping Fulham 4–1 at Craven Cottage before hammering Brentford 5–1, who were the only team to do the double over Man City (winning both home and away) that season. A draw against Man United at Old Trafford should have been a win, with Joelinton missing a sitter as De Gea was spreadeagled on the floor. After that, we won three in a row, against Everton, Spurs and Villa. We were absolutely flying and it was brilliant to see what an unbelievable transformation Eddie Howe had inspired, not just on the pitch but around the city as well. That month, we were unbeaten, winning five out of six games, earning Eddie his second Manager of the Month award since joining the club. It proved to be a triple celebration for the club, because Almirón, who'd had an utterly spectacular month, scored six goals in six games, winning the Player of the Month award as well as the Goal of the Month for his stunning first goal against Fulham on 1 October. That goal prompted Eddie to say afterwards: 'I'm delighted for [him]; he's such an infectious character. His work sort of epitomises our play, so it was great to see … He's capable of doing magical things, and for me [his first goal] was a magical goal.' Almirón was a completely different player, so what was the magic formula this time?

I think the first thing Eddie did was give Almirón a clear vision of what he wanted from him. Under Steve Bruce, you got the sense he was never sure what he was going to be asked to do or where he'd be playing. Eddie has sharpened his focus. The coaching team clearly spent time making sure Miggy was in the right place at the right time when he received the ball and worked on his finishing and timing his forward runs. He's also responded really well to the team's shape on the pitch. The team confidently carry the ball forward from the back much more under Eddie Howe, and that means Almirón can receive the ball higher up the pitch and use his pace to cause the opposition problems. Also, when you've got the kind of quality that Bruno has brought to the team in terms of distribution, your forward players are going to benefit, and nobody benefited more than Almirón in that opening half of the season. Miggy had also linked up superbly with Kieran Trippier, Joelinton and Callum Wilson. In February 2023, he was rewarded for his hard work and fantastic performances with a new three-and-a-half-year deal, which brought out that trademark smile as he was snapped putting pen to paper. Afterwards he acknowledged how hard he's worked to improve his levels and was full of praise for the coaching staff and his teammates for their help.

I asked Eddie in June 2023 how he'd achieved such a transformation in players like Almirón. He told me: 'The training is hard work but the players hopefully see the positive results of that. I'm a firm believer that you train how you play or you play how you train. We ask a lot but it's all for their benefit so that on matchday they can give a good account of themselves and show their true abilities. That process happened during the first season when we were battling relegation. We were slow to mould our playing style. I think you've seen a truer representation of that this season. And then you've seen some players really blossom in that environment. We've got some really good athletes in the team that have shown their physical capabilities, with the likes of Sean Longstaff, Joelinton, Miguel Almirón – their performances have grown, their confidence has grown and their physical outputs have just been huge and they've all benefited from that playing style.'

Eddie is seriously invested in his players' development and long-term futures. And as a man manager who genuinely cares about his players as people, he treats each of them differently, taking into account that they've all had different upbringings, histories and difficulties to overcome. He naturally becomes a second father to them. It's a key characteristic he shares with Sir Bobby Robson, whose former players from George Burley to Gazza and Ronaldo often went on the record describing Sir Bobby as 'their second father'. Eddie has also, in terms of dealing with long-term injury, overcoming personal grief and becoming a father while working practically 24/7 in football, *been there*. He doesn't have to put himself in someone else's shoes. He's literally worn those shoes. All of these attributes and experiences come together to give Eddie the compassion, foresight and emotional intelligence to help his players at various points in their lives. For example, he developed a plan in advance to help Bruno when he became a father for the first time in October 2022. In an interview with Sky Sports in mid-October 2022, Bruno said of Eddie: 'For me, he is like an English father. We have a great relationship. We speak about everything … He is a good guy, a person I really love to work with and be with.'

You could feel the sense of togetherness and support amongst his teammates when Bruno returned to the squad two days after the birth of his son to face Spurs away on 23 October 2022, which we won 2–1, lifting us into the Champions League places for the first time that season. In a post-match interview, Bruno said: 'It's been incredible. I've had two days without sleep. I would stay home, but I love to be here with these guys. They make me happy and proud, and I think we deserved it today.' This sentiment was echoed by what Callum Wilson had to say about Bruno after the game: 'We're so happy for him. He's an emotional guy, and it's been an emotional few days, and we topped it off today.'

November began where October left off with a big 4–1 away win at Southampton, followed by a 1–0 win at St James' Park against Chelsea. That victory was a massive moment. Although Chelsea hadn't performed well that season, it was right before the 2022 World Cup and the atmosphere at St James' Park was fantastic. The goal took a while to come but when it did it was a belter, Joe Willock firing into the top corner from the edge of the box after a great run from Miggy, before knee-sliding towards the corner flag in front of the Gallowgate End. It felt like a seismic moment in the season. I actually ran into club co-owners Amanda Staveley and Mehrdad Ghodoussi at the bottom of the escalators in the Milburn Stand and gave them both a hug. Amanda, who always wears her heart on her sleeve, was overcome with emotion at both the performance and the atmosphere. We all were – it felt like a huge win. At Christmas 2022, we were third in the table. Toon-mad Geordies could relax and probably enjoy the best Christmas they'd had in 20 years. The World Cup was underway and Nick Pope, Kieran Trippier and Callum Wilson were all heading to Qatar with England. It was the first time since 1998 that three Newcastle United players had been named in an England World Cup squad (Glenn Hoddle named Alan Shearer, Rob Lee and David Batty in his squad for France 98) and it was yet further testament that we were getting back towards those 'glory (ish) days' of the mid-nineties.

In the new year, we went to the Emirates to face Arsenal. Unusually for us, we set ourselves up to defend against a top-of-the-table Arsenal team and we were the happier of the teams with a 0–0 scoreline. Mikel Arteta, the Arsenal boss, was fuming during the game about penalty decisions that went against him and was complaining about time-wasting. It was the first game that they'd lost points in at home all season, and if they had won, they would have been 10 points clear of Man City. After the game, Eddie was asked by a journalist about going to Arsenal, Liverpool and Spurs that season, 'ruffling a few feathers on and off the pitch' and whether Newcastle are perceived differently now. This was Eddie's reply: 'I think I've said before: we're not here to be popular and to get other teams to like us. We're here to compete. And to compete you have to give everything to try and get a positive result. I've got no issue saying that. That's our job and that's what we're going to try and do.'

It was a proud moment as a fan of Newcastle United. It was a warning shot across the bows to every team in the Premier

League. We weren't here to make up the numbers any more. We were competitive, we were combative and we believed we could win against anyone.

Not everything went to plan after that game, though. We faced League One's Sheffield Wednesday away in the FA Cup and spurned a whole host of chances, losing 2–1 to the Owls. Eddie had taken the opportunity to shuffle the pack a little and give some squad players a run out. It backfired though and it was perhaps a reminder that our squad depth would need a bit of work if we were going to try and compete on numerous fronts in the seasons ahead. It was also the first time I'd actually wanted VAR because some of the decisions in the game were baffling, but without the help of the video assistant referee in the FA Cup, they were allowed to stand. It was a disappointing day in many ways because it meant one of our genuine trophy-winning opportunities had slipped away at the first hurdle.

We had to bounce back because the next game was a really big one, against Leicester in the quarter-finals of the Carabao Cup. Winning this one would be a big deal – we hadn't made it through to the semi-finals of the League Cup since 1976. We were bolstered by Isak's return from injury and we came all guns blazing into that game, very nearly scoring inside the first minute. Somehow it was 0–0 at half-time, but we kept pressing and who should step up but local hero Dan Burn, collecting a pass from Joelinton, driving into the box between two defenders and curling past Ward into the bottom corner. It was his first goal for the club and what a goal it was. The entire stadium erupted

into a chorus of 'He's From Blyth' and there was a party atmosphere forming under the floodlights. The icing on the cake was
provided by two players Eddie had transformed: Almirón sending
a perfectly weighted ball into the path of Joelinton who hit it first
time into the corner in front of the Gallowgate End. It was an
emphatic performance and showed the resilience Eddie had built
into our players – the memory of the cupset at Hillsborough just
three days before could have been a year ago. We were into the
Carabao Cup semi-final. Get in there!

Eddie's post-match dressing-room talk was filmed, and it
went like this: 'Life and football is about moments. There's two
moments that I want you to reflect on today. The first one is
the final whistle. We're through to the semi-final of a major cup
competition. Fantastic. The second is Dan Burn's goal in front
of the Gallowgate End.' Cue some outrageous dance moves from
Dan Burn in front of the camera and a team pic. The atmosphere
in that dressing room 'was wonderful', as Emile Heskey said
afterwards. You could see how close the players were. It brought
a big smile to every fan's face. This is what Luke Edwards of the
Daily Telegraph said of the quarter-final win:

'There has been a lot of pain, a lot of frustration, during
those dark, dreary years of underachievement. But this is a new
Newcastle and it was in front of a seething, swaying mass of black
and white in the stands. A giant is not stirring, it is sitting bolt
upright and looks ready to go on a rampage.'

In the next league game, we finally found a way through a
stubborn Fulham defence in the 89th minute, Sean Longstaff

finding Callum Wilson at the far post who nodded it back across goal to find Isak unmarked. What a way to announce your return to the Premier League after injury, scoring the winner at the Gallowgate End at the death. It also felt like we'd done what really good teams do – get a result even when you haven't played your best. We were proving how mentally strong we'd become under Eddie Howe.

In the January transfer window, the big signing for us was young winger Anthony Gordon joining us from Everton on 29 January 2023. He was all smiles, shaking hands with everyone he saw in the training ground. When players are signed by the club, they watch a presentation about the club's history, the fans, the area and the club's ambition. On the screen before the presentation starts is a heading that reads 'Start of a New Era' with two inspiring quotes beneath it, one from Amanda Staveley that reads: 'We want the same ambition as Man City and Paris Saint-Germain in terms of trophies, absolutely.' Underneath that is one from Eddie Howe: 'The pull of the club is huge, the size of the club, the history of the club. I've been very impressed with their vision for the club.'

After that, Anthony goes into the manager's office to meet Eddie. He's overwhelmingly positive, telling the player how much both he and the coaching staff have admired him. The hours of analysis that have gone in behind the scenes is quite extraordinary but it's one of the key reasons that Eddie is gathering together such an impressive record when it comes to new signings. The whole set-up at the football club – the recruitment department, the analysis team, the backroom staff – all want to make sure their new signing is the perfect fit.

Eddie was characteristically modest to me about the success of the new signings since his first January transfer window in 2021 brought Kieron Trippier, Bruno and Dan Burn to the club: 'It's not usual you get such a high percentage right on recruitment and we're aware of that. We don't want that to stop and we're not going to have endless funds. It's going to be tight and we're going to be smart and try and get more right than we get wrong. I never make any promises with anything because you can't, but the work will go in before we sign any player and we'll try to minimise the mistakes through hard work.'

It almost feels like the Financial Fair Play restrictions that Eddie alludes to play to his strengths that he forged when Bournemouth were hit with a transfer embargo, had no money to play with and were deducted points. It's helped him spot potential and hone his meticulous attention to detail. But it also helps bring about a unique 'we're in this together' mentality that drives them forward in adversity, inspires everyone around him to go the extra mile and fills them with hope for the future. And that's reflected in the words that are emblazoned on the dressing-room wall: 'The power to lift, to inspire, to achieve'.

The end of the transfer window coincided with the second leg of the semi-final of the Carabao Cup against Southampton. We'd beaten them away in the first leg 1–0 after Joelinton sprinted to meet a pinpoint Isak cross to fire home. When we score in a big away game in front of our fans, it does feel like St James'

Park travels with us. The noise, the passion – it's incredible. The second leg, at St James', again we came out of the blocks at sprint pace and didn't let up. Just four minutes in, Sean Longstaff picked up the ball in the box after a nice bit of work by Trippier, took a touch, and hammered a low drive into the corner. And Longstaff was there again in the box 15 minutes later to meet Almirón's pull-back across goal to send the Gallowgate End wild. 'I've never played in an atmosphere like that before. I was just saying to Longy before the game, "I could feel myself getting emotional," because the players were bouncing,' Dan Burn said to Sky Sports afterwards. Man of the match Sean Longstaff said to talkSPORT: 'The manager has come in and turned a lot of careers around and a lot of us will be forever grateful to him. We work hard every day to get better and better … we love working with him and will be forever grateful to him.'

. . .

Unfortunately, the one inevitable sticky run we had in the season came at exactly the wrong moment in February, with two draws (against West Ham at home and Bournemouth away) and a loss against Liverpool. That was our build-up to the Carabao Cup final, which wasn't ideal. Also, it coincided with our opponents in the final, Man United, winning three of their previous four league games and not conceding against Leeds away or Leicester at home. When we got to the final, beating Southampton in the semi-final 3–1 on aggregate and knowing who we were up against in the final, Newcastle United fans said the same thing: we're better than they are.

When Nick Pope got sent off for handling the ball outside his area in the Premier League game against Liverpool on 18 February 2023, you could see he was absolutely disconsolate. He knew what it meant instantly – that he'd be suspended for the Carabao Cup final. As luck would have it, our second-choice keeper, Martin Dúbravka, was cup-tied for the game having played on loan for Man United that season. So the number 1 jersey went to our third keeper, Loris Karius, who'd signed for us on 12 September 2022. This was his first game for the club. His last game for a Premier League club had been for Liverpool in the Champions League final of 2018 against Real Madrid, which Liverpool lost 3–1. That was, I'm afraid to say, a calamitous night for Karius, first when he tried to roll the ball out, only for Karim Benzema to block it with an outstretched right boot and send the ball agonisingly into the net. That was a howler, but what followed was an even louder one, flapping at Gareth Bale's speculative effort from 35 yards and letting the ball slip through his fingers. In fairness to Karius, he was diagnosed with concussion five days later by doctors in Boston, USA, and the suspected cause of the injury could well have been an elbow to the side of the head from Sergio Ramos early on in the game. But, either way, his debut for Newcastle United would be in the Carabao Cup final, which was a massive test for him. I felt nervous for Karius, so God knows how he must have been feeling.

In keeping with Eddie Howe's respect and reverence for legendary past players and managers, he asked Alan Shearer to talk to the players before the Carabao Cup final in the dressing room. Here's what Eddie said about his decision:

'He's been excellent, he cares about Newcastle, he wants the club to be successful and naturally if he can help that process, he will. He was really good on the week of the cup final; we had him in and he spoke absolutely brilliantly. Didn't help us get the result (!) but he more than played his part in settling the lads down and getting us to prepare properly for that match.'

Alan told me about the talk he gave in the build-up to the final: 'It was very nice and very kind of him – a great gesture being asked in. I didn't know whether to do it or not to be honest, without being disrespectful, because a lot of the players there knew me more off television than from when I was playing. But I really enjoyed going in and they were great. It was just a shame that Newcastle had that three-week period where they had a bit of a blip and one or two things went against them. Any other time during the season and the result would have been different. It was just that period, every club has it and Newcastle had theirs just when they didn't need it.'

Even though the circumstances leading up to the match weren't great, the excitement of the fans was on another level. The clamour to get hold of tickets was absolutely off the scale as well. I'm not exaggerating when I say that at least 200 people asked me if I could help them through various mediums. People I'd not heard from in years and lots of people I'd never even met. To be honest I don't mind all that. I just focus on the fact that I would have been exactly the same. I'd have tried absolutely everything I could to get tickets, so fair play to everyone that did. In the end I managed to get a pair, so my son Will was able to join me for the big day, but unfortunately my mum and dad missed out through the ballot. I think they were just happy that their son and grandson would be there, so in some way our family was represented in Wembley Stadium on such a potentially historic day. All sorts was going on in the lead-up to the game. The Toon Army had attached a massive football shirt to the Angel of the North with the words 'Howay the Lads 2023 Wembley'. Fronts of shops had been redecorated with black-and-white flags and posters. All anybody could talk about or focus on was whether or not Newcastle United's long wait for a trophy was about to come to an end. The day before the game, London was awash with black and white, with loads of fans getting together in Trafalgar Square for an all-nighter. One of the most emotional moments was my friend and colleague Keith Downie interviewing a silver-haired Geordie outside Wembley who told him he was really nervous. 'Sixty years since I started following Newcastle and it's in the blood. It's really in the blood,' he said. When Keith asked him if he was confident Newcastle would get over the line, he said: 'Not bothered. We're here. It's the start of the journey and we're going.' I still occasionally watch that clip back and it always makes me feel emotional. I've waited my whole life to see Newcastle United win a trophy, but there are plenty out there who have waited even longer.

On the morning of the game I woke like a kid at Christmas. I had a really strong feeling in my stomach that this was going to be our year. I had my son Will alongside me and he was going to live a life full of trophies and success and this was the start.

My head was full of memories of trudging down Wembley Way full of tears, sadness and regret from my own youth, but Will's memories would be ones of joy and celebration. I'd decided not to drink alcohol in the build-up. Mainly because I had my son with me, but also because I really wanted to live and breathe every moment and not have the experience clouded by the effects of a few beers. In reality it was lucky that I made that decision because once we made our way into the stadium I couldn't move for supporters wanting a chat and a photo. The excitement levels were off the scale and some had clearly not been to bed for a couple of days and were cooking on fumes, but as always everybody was absolutely spot on with both little Gravesy and me. Sadly, despite the incredible scenes as the players emerged from the tunnel, to a sea of black-and-white flags and banners, the reality is we didn't play like we knew we could and it was a big disappointment, but a first Wembley final for us since 1998 was some achievement.

And it was such a welcome change after the Ashley era of not prioritising the cup competitions, which he perceived to be less lucrative. During that time, it became a running joke among fans that we'd be out of both cups in the third round. But we were back, competing with the best. An emotional Amanda Staveley said to talkSPORT after the final: 'I was crying, my son was crying, we're all crying. But it was amazing, at 2–0 down, we had flags going. The passion from everyone, they've taken us on this journey. This is all about the amazing fans who have taken us on this amazing journey. We're just honoured and humbled. We feel very privileged to run Newcastle.' My son and I were amongst the last people to leave the stadium. Will was really upset. He looked dejected as we stood in silence watching the Man United players lift the trophy. He reminded me so much of myself when I was young and that dreaded feeling of 'it's all over' pounding around in your heart and mind. I tapped him on the shoulder and said, 'Guess what, mate. We're fourth in the Premier League.' He smiled and replied, 'Yeah, that's a good point to be fair, Dad.' And with that I took his hand and we left. I'm certain it won't be another 20 years before we're back.

We had to recover from that emotionally draining final and face another ridiculously tough test the following week. This time it was a trip to Man City in the league and probably the last thing we needed after the heartbreak of Wembley. We didn't play that badly but we still lost 2–0. Phil Foden scored a fantastic solo goal after just 15 minutes, cutting in from the right, and holding off two players, before his effort took a wicked deflection off Sven Botman's outstretched leg and wrong-footed Nick Pope. Just moments later, Nathan Aké made a crucial block to deny Sean Longstaff from close range. We were a constant threat after that, but miscues from Wilson and Joelinton on the edge of the six-yard line cost us. It came down to the age-old trope: they converted their chances, we didn't. Bernardo Silva came off the bench and put the game to bed on 67 minutes, lashing a quick left-footed shot into the bottom corner from the edge of the area. It could have been a different result had we taken one of our second-half chances. Pep Guardiola was full of praise for our performance afterwards, indicating that we'd be a title threat over the next few years. But in truth, it was the low spell of the season – we'd gone eight games without a win, and in that time, we'd only found the net on three occasions.

In the next game against Wolves, it could have been a different story had Nick Pope been sent off after 20 minutes for a clumsy challenge on Raúl Jiménez in the penalty area that had me wincing when I saw the replay. But we rode our luck with that one and then capitalised six minutes later with a superb free kick from Kieran Trippier that was met by an equally superb leap and header from Isak that arrowed into the bottom corner past keeper José Sá. Wolves could have easily gone two down after a fantastic corner from Trippier again and a Longstaff knock-back that Bruno clattered against the crossbar. But they rallied after that, Daniel Podence hitting the post from the edge of the box and Pope pulling out a top-drawer save to stop a powerful Pedro Neto strike from a well-worked indirect free kick. Trippier went close from a free kick of his own in the second half that threatened to beat Sá at his near post, but the keeper covered his ground. Trippier, who'd had an otherwise blinding game, was at fault after 70 minutes, slipping while trying to clear the ball and gifting a tap-in to Hwang Hee-chan who couldn't believe his luck. But we pressed for a winner and were rewarded nine minutes later, Joe Willock sliding a perfect through-ball to Almirón who found a way past Sá via a deflection. The truth is we'd been a little fortunate but it felt no less than we deserved after not getting the rub of the green in the past few matches. It was a vital, confidence-building victory.

The next game away at Nottingham Forest was a memorable one. We hit the crossbar twice in the first half before Botman's back-pass was cut out by Emmanuel Dennis who coolly chipped it into the net. We found a way back at the end of the first half with an incredible improvised finish from Isak off his outstretched shin. It was an outrageous goal, really, and didn't even look possible. We had a goal ruled out for offside midway through the second half that would have been Elliot Anderson's first for the club, after a teasing looped cross from Isak found Anderson in the box. At first no one had any idea why it was even being reviewed but Sean Longstaff was deemed to be offside in the build-up. It was ridiculous really, because Forest defender Felipe had deliberately tried to send the ball out of play, which would have played Longstaff onside. Fortunately, that didn't prove to be decisive in the outcome of the game because we were awarded a penalty in injury time after a handball from Moussa Niakhaté. In one of my favourite moments of the season, Kieran Trippier picked up the ball and stood over the spot while all hell was breaking loose around him and in the stands. You can imagine the mind games that were at play with defenders and so on telling him he was going to miss. But Tripps just stood there with a wry grin on his face. Then amazingly at the very last second he handed the ball to the towering figure of Alexander Isak, who stepped up, cool as you like, and slotted the ball into the top corner in front of the Newcastle United end. Cue wild celebrations from the Toon Army behind the goal. It was a great penalty, but more than that a moment of incredible leadership from Trippier who took all the pressure away from the young Swedish striker. It's stuff like that which makes this team so wonderfully loveable to watch as a fan. But Eddie deserves a lot of credit for that, identifying and honing Trippier's leadership qualities and encouraging the other leaders in the group to calm everyone down at difficult moments. That win was a big result, not least because it was the first time we'd come from behind to win a Premier League game that season.

The Premier League took a break towards the end of March while the first games of Euro 24 qualifying took place. Eddie took the players and staff to Dubai, which was a good opportunity for our new signings – Anthony Gordon and Harrison Ashby (who joined from West Ham for £3 million on 31 January 2023), as well as players like Emil Krafth who were recovering from long-term injuries – to spend some quality time around the squad and integrate properly into the group. Eddie reflected intelligently on that aspect of the trip, telling NUFC TV that, 'It sometimes takes a trip away to actually feel fully at home.' Of the benefits of the rest period itself, Eddie said: 'It gives us a chance for the first few days to just unwind slightly because the rigours of the Premier League, the stresses of the PL, if you're at that engaged and high-alert state all the time it's not actually good for you. We've tried to bring them down but also you can stay down for too long, so it's getting that balance right, where now we bring the lads back to work and make sure their bodies are fully conditioned for the next game.'

And they'd need to be in the best possible shape for the next game, because it was against Man United at St James' Park and we had a score to settle. Not only was it in the wake of the Carabao Cup final defeat, but we were also sitting just two places below them in the league, in fifth, three points away.

After a dominant first-half display, it seemed like one of those games where we just wouldn't be able to find the net. De Gea stopped everything that came at him. But then Isak played a spectacular ball through to Bruno who looped an inviting cross over for Saint-Maximin to lay up perfectly for Joe Willock to nod in. And we deserved it. We were quicker, we were stronger and we were hungrier. Callum Wilson made sure that every Geordie would head home with a smile on their face when he leapt highest to meet a beautiful curling ball in from Trippier. Cue absolute pandemonium at St James' Park. Dan Burn said afterwards to Sky Sports: 'It's really special ... we owed them one this season.'

The Sky Sports cameras captured part of Eddie's speech to the players in the dressing room straight after the game:

'For me we got what we deserved today because of how we've trained in the last two weeks. In the last two weeks our attitude and application to everything we've asked you to do has been top. Very, very pleased with everybody in the room. We move on because we've got another game very, very quickly, so make sure we're professional in the next couple of days and we need to try and get this feeling again throughout the week. Three games in six days is a big ask. Our confidence levels should be through the roof after that. We'll build on it guys, well done.'

The confidence coursed through the team after that, and you could see it in the early stages of the next game against West

Ham at the London Stadium. It only took six minutes to break the deadlock, Saint-Maximin with some great work down the left, expertly finding an unmarked Wilson who powered a header into the far corner. And a delighted Wilson launched straight into the Macarena, which we later learned was honouring a bet he'd made with friend and Footballer's Football Podcast co-host Michail Antonio. Whichever of them scored would have to bust out the moves. Just seven minutes later, Joelinton danced past Fabiański and slid the ball home after a ball forward from Fabian Schär from well inside our own half tore the Hammers defence in half. It was immediately disallowed for offside by the assistant referee but VAR overturned it, clearly showing that left-back Emerson was playing him onside. Zouma nodded in from a corner to make it 2–1 near the end of the first half, but any chance of a West Ham fightback was snuffed out after a dreadful defensive lapse gifted Wilson a second. It was the same story for our third, this time Fabiański horribly misjudging an attempted clearance, but Isak had some work to do from 30 yards out, chesting it before calmly and skilfully lobbing a volley into the empty net. Joelinton completed a 5–1 thrashing with a fine finish after some pretty woeful defending, again. We'd won four Premier League games on the bounce. We were sitting in third place in the table on 53 points, level with Man United on points but well above them on goal difference. Spurs were three points behind and we had a game in hand, with Brighton another four points back in sixth. Europe was fast becoming a realistic outcome, but I don't think any of us had dared to dream that far ahead just yet. However, the signs were looking good.

The next game, away at Brentford, was tough from the start. Brentford started brightly and Ivan Toney had the ball in the net early on but VAR confirmed he was just offside. Just before the half-hour mark, Botman took out Brentford forward Kevin Schade but Toney's tame penalty was gratefully gobbled up by Nick Pope. It was his first miss in 25 spot-kicks, and the crowd was stunned. But Toney got a chance to redeem himself after Brentford were awarded another penalty, this time via VAR, as Isak was judged to have fouled Rico Henry. Toney made no mistake this time. We were much better in the second half and when Joelinton ghosted from out wide into the six-yard box, keeper David Raya could only turn his effort into the net. On the hour mark, Joelinton found Wilson on the edge of the area who teed up Isak to curl in a stunning effort into the top corner. We saw out an uncomfortable closing 15 minutes after that but held on for the win against a strong side pushing for Europe themselves. It was our fifth straight league win, and Isak was looking untouchable.

We were confident but we faced a tricky away match at Aston Villa, who'd been on quite a run of their own, with six wins in seven league appearances under new manager Unai Emery. It was the first game in the whole season where I felt we were outplayed. We were nearly blown away in the first 20 minutes, if truth be told, and 3–0 to Villa felt quite kind on us at full-time. Eddie acknowledged as much on *Match of the Day* after the game.

In the next game at home to Spurs, you wouldn't have known we'd been beaten in the previous game. It was a day that none of my family will ever forget. We'd been invited to the game that day by one of the sponsors, so it was going to be a special day out and a rare trip to St James' Park for my wife Steph and our two daughters Poppy and Daisy. When we arrived we were told that one of the other guest's kids was due to be mascot for the day but hadn't been able to make the match, so would any of my lot be able to step in as a last-minute substitute. Obviously our football mad son, Will, got the opportunity, although I'd have given anything to be 30 years younger and done it myself. Within minutes he was handed a football kit and taken down to the tunnel to stand with the players. To see little Gravesy walk out beside Fabian Schär was a surreal and brilliant moment for us all. It must be incredible to see your child emerge as an actual player, but incredibly nerve-wracking as well. Luckily, Gravesy was able to leave the field before the game began, but if he'd known how bad Spurs were going to be, he probably would have begged to stay on.

Eddie had galvanised belief among the squad that a setback would do nothing to hurt our confidence or attack-mindedness. And now it was our turn to completely annihilate a team in the first 20 minutes. We were sensational from the whistle, pushing forward immediately, with Joelinton cutting in and ghosting past players before forcing a good save out of Hugo Lloris that Jacob Murphy was much more alive to than Ivan Perišić, smashing home from a tight angle. Barely four minutes later, we'd barely taken our seats before a long ball forward from Schär split both centre-backs and found Joelinton who took it down perfectly and calmly went round Lloris. The Gallowgate End went absolutely mental. Spurs were there for the taking and we kept pushing forward. Jacob Murphy found himself in space 30 yards out and wasn't being closed down, so unleashed a long-range drive that found the bottom left corner. Murphy's face afterwards was priceless. He looked as stunned as everyone else in the ground. Three goals in nine minutes. It was one of those 'I was there' moments.

But it was about to get even better and even louder, as Joe Willock produced one of the best passes I've ever seen. A sensational 45-yard, outside of the boot looping pass that fell perfectly into the path of a sprinting Alexander Isak, who slotted into the far corner to make it 4–0 on 19 minutes. And the next time we went forward, we scored again, a terrific interchange of passes finding Isak who lashed home past Lloris. His facial expression summed it up. He held his hands up and twisted his face as if to say, 'What on earth is happening here?' and he was right. It was 5–0 after 20 minutes. No one had ever seen anything like it at St James' Park. In the celebrations that followed the fifth goal I turned around and made eye contact with music icon Sting who was also celebrating a few rows behind me. I'm not sure why that's relevant, but it merely added to the surreal nature of the whole afternoon. Just after the break, Harry Kane got his traditional goal for Spurs, after a great bit of solo work, but he didn't celebrate it. Isak and Murphy came off after 66 minutes, more than earning an early bath, and were replaced by Callum Wilson and Miguel Almirón. Within a matter of seconds, these two combined to allow Wilson to side-foot goal number six past Lloris. We'd had 25 shots in that game, eight of which were on target, but we'd scored with six of them. The crowd was bouncing and a big mention goes to Jacob Murphy who had his best performance in a Newcastle shirt. We were utterly dominant and up to third in the table, six points clear of fifth-placed Spurs and with a game in hand with just seven games left to play. That match against Spurs was a game-changer because it cemented the belief that the Champions League was on for us. This season, we weren't just breaking apart the so-called 'Big Six' teams – we were breaking the rule book by comfortably sitting in the top four.

Murphy's transformation also had everything to do with Eddie Howe's man management and incredible tailored improvement plan. Murphy signed for Newcastle under Rafa Benítez in July 2017 for an undisclosed fee from Norwich City. It was a dream come true for a lad who'd grown up as a Toon fan and described Alan Shearer as 'a god'. Although he was born in London, both his parents are from either side of Newcastle, and his first game at St James' Park was a UEFA Cup win against PSV Eindhoven. He didn't become a regular first-team player, though, and spent most of the time coming on as a sub or warming the bench. I remember when fans on the terraces were saying that Rafa had bought the wrong Murphy twin* when they saw some of Jacob Murphy's performances in the 2017–18 season. He'd gone out on loan in early 2019 at West Brom for eight months before spending the whole of the 2019–20 season on

* His twin brother Josh also started at Norwich before going to Cardiff in 2018 and Oxford United in 2022.

loan at Sheffield Wednesday. He returned to us for the 2020–21 season but when Eddie took over in November 2021, it didn't seem as though he was really going to feature. He made a handful of starts in the first four months after Eddie took over but again mostly found himself being subbed on for short spells.

An opportunity presented itself when Almirón went down with a thigh injury in March 2023 and Murphy started the next seven games, including the game against Spurs that will live long in the memory. Eddie's given him clear focus and played him in a more attacking role, which has worked out really well for him and the team. He was in the form of his life and it must have pleased him no end when his run of performances drew praise from Alan Shearer (alongside Almirón and Fabian Schär) for their 'colossal improvement' in May 2023. Now, it feels like Murphy is an important part of the current squad. It's been another incredible transformation under Howe.

We picked up where we left off in the next match away at Everton, with Joelinton causing all sorts of problems down the left, checking back and sending a curling right-footed effort which Pickford could only parry towards Callum Wilson, who was the first to the rebound. Willock was unlucky not to score a stunning volley from the edge of the area, which Pickford just managed to get his fingertips to. And it was Willock's darting run and delicate chip from the byline which laid it on a plate for Joelinton to head in. Wilson still had more in the tank, wrapping his foot around the ball with no backlift to curl in a beauty to the far right corner which Pickford could do nothing about. Everton got one back from a corner before Isak produced one of the moments of the season, not just for Newcastle, but in the Premier League. He took the ball from near the halfway line on the far left, sprinted past two defenders before jinking this way and that with some sublime footwork to beat three players, advance along the byline and lay it on a plate for Jacob Murphy. 'That's a real thing of beauty,' Eddie said afterwards before acknowledging that Isak did share similarities with Premier League legend Thierry Henry: 'He's certainly got the speed and is a similar build and frame. The footwork for the assist against Everton was truly remarkable really. The amount of turns and twists and step overs he did, an incredible piece of skill. He has incredible ball manipulation.'

Against Southampton, in the next match, Isak and Wilson combined superbly for our first goal after the Saints had gone ahead against the run of play towards the end of the first half. After sustained pressure in the closing stages, a Trippier corner in a dangerous area came off Theo Walcott and beat keeper Alex McCarthy. Callum Wilson then made no mistake after a long ball broke nicely for him, skipping past the keeper to slot it in at the Gallowgate End to make it 3–1. It was his 15th goal of the season.

There was a lot at stake in our home game against Arsenal, who'd topped the table for almost the entire season but had finally been overhauled by an unstoppable Man City side at the beginning of May 2023. But we started the stronger of the two teams, Jacob Murphy clattering a low drive against the post before we were awarded a penalty for a suspected handball which was overturned by VAR. Minutes later, Martin Ødegaard squeezed a 30-yard strike into the corner. Willock should have equalised after the ball broke kindly for him in the area, but he shot straight at a grateful Aaron Ramsdale. Ødegaard pulled out a good stop from Pope before Isak hit the post with a header after an excellent dink of a cross from Murphy. A Trippier free kick found Fabian Schär, but his strong header was denied by an equally strong reaction stop from Ramsdale. We were guilty of squandering our chances, and we were made to rue them when Gabriel Martinelli's low corner was inadvertently turned into his own net by Schär. It had been a pulsating match and, to be honest, it could have gone either way.

It was all going on at Elland Road in a bruising encounter with Leeds under temporary manager Sam Allardyce that featured three penalties and a sending-off. Wilson scored twice from the spot in the match and the game looked won in the middle of the second half before a lucky deflection off Trippier gave Leeds an equaliser. But a 2–2 result against a team fighting for survival was a decent result, in my view at least.

Five days later, we were hosting a strong Brighton side who were pushing for the Europa League places. They'd just beaten Arsenal 3–0 away, so we were in no doubt about the threat they posed. A fantastic inswinging corner from Trippier was flicked into his own net by Deniz Undav in the middle of the first half, and Dan Burn rose highest to meet another top-quality Trippier delivery, this one from a free kick, to make it 2–0 on the stroke of half-time. The Seagulls found themselves a lifeline early on in the second half after a through ball was met by Undav who held his nerve to beat Pope. It took until the last couple of minutes to make sure of the points – a terrific run and defence-splitting pass from Almirón found Wilson in acres of space and he did what he'd done for most of the season, slotting past their keeper in front of a rapturous Gallowgate End. We weren't going to sit back on our lead – we kept pushing forward and another incisive ball forward found Wilson who held the ball up superbly before unselfishly squaring it for the onrushing Bruno to lash it past Jason Steele. What an unbelievable moment that was and the roof nearly lifted off the stadium again. That win left us on the verge of an unthinkable achievement at the beginning of the season: Champions League football. All we needed in our next game, four days later, was a point against Leicester.

That final home game was a strange one in many ways. The build-up had felt pretty spectacular. You could hear the Champions League anthem being played from pubs on the walk up to the stadium. Once we got inside, there was the usual sea of black-and-white flags and noise, but then the East Stand unfurled an incredible gigantic banner of Eddie Howe and the whole squad (put together by Wor Flags) that almost stretched the entire length of the pitch. Leicester's game plan seemed to be to soak up the pressure for the entire game, put 11 men behind the ball and hope for a miracle on the break. And they very nearly got it. But we should have been comfortably two or three up by that point. We controlled the game, with 78 per cent possession, Wilson hitting the post in the middle of the first half and having his follow-up cleared off the line. Almirón struck the post three minutes before half-time, with Isak send-ing the rebound just over the top. We peppered the goal in the second half but nothing was sticking. And then, in injury time at the end of the game, Nick Pope, who might as well have been sitting in a deckchair for 90 minutes, was called on to make a stunning save to keep out an acrobatic effort from Timothy Castagne. The final whistle blew and that moment undoubtedly produced the biggest cheer of the night. In many ways it felt like a disappointing result but in reality it didn't matter. The reality of the achievement sank in while 'Que Sera Sera' rang around the stadium. We'd qualified for the Champions League with a game to spare. There were beaming smiles on the pitch and in the stands. The players did a lap of honour, joined by their fami-lies, with the players' kids kicking balls around. I weaved my way down to join my mum and dad in the heart of the Milburn Stand. The chairman hugged Eddie and the players on the pitch and they all posed for a group photo. They were unbelievable scenes to celebrate an unforgettable moment.

Eddie spoke after the match to the press and was asked a question about whether he ever envisaged bringing the kind of unity to Newcastle United that was on show at the Leicester game. Here's what he said:

'What I felt we could try and galvanise was the supporter base, that we could bring that connection between the players and the supporters every time we entered the pitch, but it would take a huge effort from us to deliver that and when I say 'us', it's the players. The players have to go out and show what it means to represent this city every time they play, and I think they have done. I think we've produced a really hard-working, passionate group of players that understand what it means to represent this club and what the supporters expect is that you go out and give your best every time you put the shirt on.'

Two players that had certainly achieved that was our centre-back pairing of Fabian Schär and Sven Botman.

And for Schär, it was something of a rebirth because his future at Newcastle had looked in serious doubt in the autumn of 2021. Steve Bruce had him warming the bench, but things changed when Eddie Howe took charge in the first week of November. In Eddie's initial one-to-one meetings with the squad, he reportedly told Schär he would be one of his key players. Eddie had seen the promise in Schär when he was Bournemouth manager and had tried to bring him to the club in 2017 from 1899 Hoffenheim. Rafa bought him for a knock-down price after Deportivo had been relegated from La Liga in 2018 and he showed early promise, particularly with his long balls to wingers which created a quick attacking threat. But Schär slipped down the pecking order, on account of the number of errors he was making, earning him silly cards, as well as the amount of aerial battles he lost against opposition strikers. But Eddie Howe believed in him, and knew how to get the best out of him. Not only did he restore his lost confidence, he started playing him as part of a back four with a regular partner at centre-back. Schär found himself back in the starting eleven and was one of our key players.

Schär's performances in the remainder of the 2021–22 season earned him a contract extension in April 2022, with Eddie singling him out in a press conference before a game against Liverpool for being 'the ultimate professional off the pitch' and 'a big part of our leadership within the team'. He had a good season, but the numbers didn't lie: we'd shipped 62* goals in 2021–22. Only Southampton, Everton, Leeds, Watford and Norwich had conceded more than us and they'd all finished the season in the bottom six.

Eddie had a defensive plan for the 2022–23 season and he deserves a lot of credit for making an inspired signing and for the tactical brilliance we witnessed. First, he brought in Sven Botman – the ideal defensive partner for Fabian Schär. Schär does have weaknesses, but when you're complemented by 6ft 4in Sven Botman and 6ft 6in Dan Burn, you're not going to be up against their tallest, strongest offensive player. Also, he's winning the battles he's fighting – Schär was ranked fourth in the Premier League's Stats Centre for aerial battles won in 2022–23. Also, Schär's anticipation and positional placement also improved and the proof of that is that he appears equal ninth for interceptions in the Premier League's Stats Centre. In June 2023, 31-year-old Schär told Swiss news site Bluewin: 'For me it was the best and most beautiful season of my entire career. I have never felt more comfortable in a place than in Newcastle … Eddie's the best coach of my career.'

----

* In fairness, 23 of those had come before Eddie joined the club.

Schär's defensive partner, Sven Botman, had an epic first season at St James' Park. So much so that he earned a place on the shortlist for the Premier League's Young Player of the Season award. He was the only defender in that shortlist of eight (comprising our own Alexander Isak, Gabriel Martinelli, Bukayo Saka, Martin Ødegaard, Moisés Caicedo, Alexis Mac Allister and some bloke called Erling Haaland). He made key tackles, blocked shots, outmuscled attackers, calmly distributed the ball out and always seemed to be in the right place at the right time. Fans quickly began referring to him as a Rolls-Royce of a player. I think he made just one mistake in the 2022–23 season, when his flicked pass back towards Nick Pope at Nottingham Forest away in March 2023 was intercepted by the onrushing Emmanuel Dennis, who scored. Botman had just been called up to the Dutch squad under Ronald Koeman, literally the same day, and I wonder if that had affected his concentration? Either way, it was a rare error in an otherwise flawless season.

Botman bounced back immediately in the match, not allowing it to impact his confidence and it didn't end up affecting the result thanks to the Isak penalty in stoppage time, which no one celebrated more than Botman. After the game, Eddie Howe said of Botman: 'We all make mistakes – I thought he responded very well in a difficult moment. It'll be good for his learning to have gone through that.' It was a fascinating insight into the inner workings of Eddie Howe, choosing to focus on Botman's resilient response in the game and emphasising that it's vital that his players make mistakes, because in the long term they'll turn them into strengths.

Howe has brought the best out of his new signings and he's revived the careers of existing squad members. Eddie's worked tirelessly to turn all of them into fantastic assets. At St James' Park, I've got so used to hearing fans saying, 'That's the best performance I've ever seen from him in a black-and-white shirt,' every week about a different player. They're fit, chasing down everything and pressing high up the pitch to win the ball back as quickly as possible. And that's what Newcastle United fans want to see: energy, commitment and passion. Despite the fact some players are competing for the same places in the first eleven, they're fighting for each other and working towards a common goal. They're playing in a system they all believe in where everyone knows what they're doing. It's no surprise that the players believe they can win every game. And that's all down to Eddie Howe: both an inspirational manager and an exceptional coach.

To the ambitious Eddie, though, the incredible 2022–23 season seems like a building block to achieve bigger and better things. He's only just getting started. Here's how Eddie summed up the season to me and what his vision was for the future:

'I'd love to bring some silverware to Newcastle United. As I walked through the door here, that was my dream, my vision, and it hasn't changed. Top four at the end of the season doesn't come with a trophy and that's a difficult one. It's an amazing achievement and the players have been incredible and I'm not downplaying what they've achieved, but it's not a cup. That's what I'd love to do in the next stage of our development.'

The whole club is in the next stage of its development, and you could see that in action just 48 hours after the final game of the 2022–23 season. It was some massively exciting news from behind the scenes, which cemented the owners' ambitions for the club and also proved Amanda Staveley to be as good as her word. Back in late 2021, she called the training facilities at the club 'really awful', adding that 'there's no point having fantastic players if there's nowhere suitable for them to train.' Hearing her say that reminded me of the photographs that came out in October 2018 of the Ashley-era training facilities. It looked a bit like a budget holiday camp, seeing the first team cooling down in inflatable blue paddling pools and having ice baths in wheelie bins. It was pretty shocking.

But on 30 May 2023, the club released a video showing inside the new training facility hosted by club legend and current loan director at the club, Shola Ameobi. It was a nice throwback to Shola's appearance on *MTV Cribs* a few years ago, which definitely showed that the club wasn't taking itself too seriously! The new training ground is just incredible. It's completely state of the art, with hydrotherapy pools, plunge pools, a players' lounge and a restaurant overlooking the training pitches. You can also see Eddie's wheel of fortune-style fines board featuring letters A–Z that correspond to a different fine amount. It's used for players who arrive late to training or for meetings, according to Callum Wilson, and it's something he introduced at Bournemouth to 'keep everyone on their toes'. Eddie's very big on punctuality. Along the corridors of the training centre are photos taken inside the dressing room after wins in the 2022–23 season. It does everything that the words on the dressing-room wall at St James' Park say, helping lift, inspire and achieve. Finally the players don't just have a place that's fit for purpose; it's fit for the future as well.

CHAPTER 10

THE FUTURE

Being a Newcastle United fan hasn't been easy. We've had big peaks but even bigger troughs over the past 30 years on Tyneside. It's nearly always followed a familiar pattern: a messiah comes in and saves the club, but before you know it, they're gone and we enter a time of wandering through the wilderness in mourning for year after year. We desperately need to break this cycle, learn from our mistakes of the past and build something that's going to last for a long time.

While it looks like we might be on our way towards that, I think one of the most important things we can do as supporters is not to get too ahead of ourselves. During the Sir Bobby Robson era, we got into the Champions League for two seasons in a row and I'm still amazed at how quickly it became an assumption that we'd be competing at that level every single season. You think about the teams in the Premier League now competing for the Champions League places: Man City, Liverpool, Arsenal, Man United, Chelsea, Spurs and now us. Not to take anything away from the incredible season we had in 2022–23, but it's worth remembering that Chelsea had an absolutely shocking season from November onwards and finished 12th. They only scored 38 goals all season – only Wolves, Bournemouth, Everton and

Southampton scored fewer goals. Yes, it was their first season under a new owner and they seemed to be on a managerial merry-go-round, but there's no way they'll be in the bottom half of the table next season, with Mauricio Pochettino as their manager, plus a whole host of new players coming in. I expect some of their big-money signings from last season will also improve. They'll certainly pose more of a threat than before.

Spurs finished eighth, just outside the European places, for the first time in 13 years. They'll be hungrier than ever to return to the top table under new manager Ange Postecoglou and keep up with high-flying Arsenal. Liverpool underperformed in 2022–23, despite coming back strongly towards the back end of the season. They've signed World Cup winner Alexis Mac Allister from Brighton and Dominik Szoboszlai, RB Leipzig's exciting young box-to-box midfielder (who now captains Hungary), plus others, and you can't see Liverpool not being in the mix come the end of the 2023–24 season. Man United seem to be on an upward trajectory under Erik ten Hag and will be keen to build on their first trophy win since 2017. All the top clubs are upping their games, and we're going to have to do the same. Plus, we're in the Champions League (once again, how good does it feel to say that?!) for the first time in a decade, which is something Kevin Keegan had some interesting thoughts about in a chat we had in June 2023. He said, 'Newcastle have bought a raffle ticket for a tougher raffle now that they're in the Champions League; they're going to be playing on a Wednesday and a Saturday. Those games are going to come thick and fast. It's like boxing – you knock someone out and then another guy comes along who's even better than the guy you knocked out. They're in with the big boys now!'

With this in mind, I think it's really important to be level-headed about the 2023–24 Premier League season. We've had an exceptional season in 2022–23 but I'd happily take a top eight finish in 2023–24. Anything else I'd treat as a bonus. A Champions League finish isn't going to happen every year. I'm on the same page as Eddie – I'd take a Carabao Cup or an FA Cup over another top four finish next season. This club desperately needs to win some silverware. The fans deserve to celebrate a trophy and I'd be absolutely over the moon if Eddie Howe became the man to deliver it. It won't be easy. Winning the Premier League or Champions League look beyond our reach (for now at least), so it comes down to either of the English domestic cups, or perhaps the Europa League if we were to drop into that later in the season. Having said all that, I'm more optimistic than ever that if the club keeps developing in the direction it's currently travelling in, then we might just witness a Premier League title or a Champions League in my lifetime. It feels amazing to think that's now a genuine possibility somewhere down the line.

Eddie was also keen to temper fans' expectations of what the summer transfer window would look like. He emphasised in the post-match press conference at Stamford Bridge after the final game of the 2022–23 season that the squad that has performed so well in 2022–23 deserve to stay in place:

'Maybe one or two players might move this summer; it's very difficult to predict. I think we have to keep the majority of the squad together. I feel they've earned the right to do that but we have to be good in the transfer market.' This is very similar to the way he operated at Bournemouth. He likes to give the players who've earned a shot at glory the opportunity to experience that glory themselves. It makes sense to me and it's one of the reasons that this squad is so united. The players trust their manager because he simply refuses to cast them aside.

Eddie also explained that Financial Fair Play rules affect the club's potential spending and long-term approach to new signings, which I asked him about in June 2023. He told me:

'It's changed the landscape. There is a desire for Newcastle to invest, to improve very quickly, but we can't because we're tied by our income, which is on the lower side. In the future I love to think that the club will connect with various partners around the world and the income streams will go up so the club can spend more money. But at the moment that's not possible. You just have to adapt to your environment. It's been about trying to identify talent that is under the radar and as yet to blossom or show how good they are. Being adaptable and trying to pick the right players is not a science – there are so many different things that go into it. There are so many variables and you've just got to select wisely. It's a tough thing to do.'

Eddie's policy of finding young players with bags of potential has not only seen some really exciting signings – it's also a clever investment in our longer-term future. Both he and his backroom staff go to great lengths to ensure that these new acquisitions are the perfect fit, benefiting the squad as a whole.

Some of these players will go on to play five, maybe ten years with Newcastle United. Eddie's always got one eye on the bigger picture. But when I asked him about how it works, he was keen to convey that the credit for recruitment belongs to many different people at the club. So much hard work is going on behind the scenes:

'Every football club is slightly different on transfers but we've got some really good people behind the scenes – the scouting team, the recruiting department – who will churn through loads of games and come up with names. The coaching team has also got a very strong opinion and we'll sit in the office for hours churning names over and try and come up with the right solutions together. It's another really good show of how the team works. Teamwork is everything here; whether it's the scouting team, the coaching team, we all come together and try and get the right result for Newcastle United.'

The success rate is becoming one of Eddie's trademarks. You just have to mention players like Bruno, Isak, Botman, Trippier and Pope, who are well on their way to becoming club legends (or already are). But he's typically modest when I ask him about it:

'It's not usual to get such a high percentage right on recruitment and we're aware of that. We don't want that to stop and we're not going to have endless funds. It's going to be tight and we're going to be smart and try and get more right than we get wrong. I never make any promises with anything because you can't, but the work will go in before we sign any player and we'll try to minimise the mistakes through hard work.'

As for new buys, Sandro Tonali joined us on 3 July for £55 million from AC Milan, becoming the most expensive Italian export of all time. Another big money arrival was England international Harvey Barnes from Leicester City for £39 million on 23 July. Barnes joined up with the team in Philadelphia on their pre-season tour of the USA and told Chronicle Live how excited he was to start working with Eddie Howe. 'The way he speaks is so positive. You want to buy into that as a player. I have worked with him a couple of days and he is a manager you really want to work for. You want to give him that extra yard.' Barnes looks like he'll be competing with Anthony Gordon, Miguel Almirón and Jacob Murphy for a spot on the wing with Allan Saint-Maximin being sold to balance the books.

Newcastle United and Eddie Howe are always building for the future. They've spent big money to secure young full back's Tino Livramento for £32m from Southampton and Lewis Hall from Chelsea on an initial loan with an obligation to buy for £28m next summer. That's basically £60m (plus add ons) on two young lads who are both still under the age of 21. Without doubt that comes with a risk but it proves the lengths that the recruitment team at St James' Park are willing to go to to secure emerging talent. With Eddie Howe's coaching and encouragement you could easily see Livramento and Hall becoming England's first choice full back's in the next decade. The arrival of young Gambian winger Yankuba Minteh from Danish Superliga club Odense Boldklub also caught the eye. He has gone straight out on loan to Feyenoord for the season, where he will probably get some Champions League experience (all part of Eddie and Dan Ashworth's plan for the future, I have no doubt).

Signings like these prove that Newcastle United is an exciting, dynamic club led by one of the most talented, inspiring mangers in the world. As such, our perceived isolation in the North East is not proving to be the hindrance to players signing with us as it might have been in the past. The Toon Army faithful got stuck into Gabby Agbonlahor after he memorably gave his opinion on talkSPORT in November 2021, saying: 'When I was playing in the Premier League, Newcastle was the place where you weren't sure. I didn't want to go, it's far up north, the weather ... players want to be close to London, closer to London was the attraction. If you offered a player £40,000 a week at Newcastle, or £30,000 a week at Brentford, they would go to Brentford even on less money ... Players don't want to live in Newcastle,' he said, which really pi**ed off all Newcastle fans. I laughed when I heard it. I know Gabby and I thought to myself, *Probably best you don't check your social media mentions for a few days, Mr Agbonlahor*, and I was right – he got pelters.

The truth is that Newcastle is an absolutely phenomenal place to live and bring up a family. Look at me, I work full-time in London, but we chose to raise our family in Newcastle. It's an ideal location for a young footballer to move to. You only need to look at Bruno Guimarães choosing to come here in 2022. You can see how much he loves the place. After his second goal against Leicester on Boxing Day 2022, he said to The Players' Tribune: 'I ripped my shirt off, and that's when I knew that I was really in the Premier League. It was an atmosphere I'd never seen before, even in Brazil. I remember I collapsed on the pitch at the whistle and I was just praying to God, thanking him for bringing me here.' In April 2023, he said, 'I feel at home here … I'm very happy to be here to be playing and be part of this giant club's story. For me it's important and everyone knows how much I like the club, the fans, the support.'

Even though we haven't won anything for decades, Newcastle United fans always want to hear people talk about how we're a big club. The fan base, the stadium and the noise at St James' Park has always been incredible. In the minds of the fans here, Newcastle United is the biggest and best football club in the world. It's like the club is treated like an additional family member that you don't want to hear a bad word about. The city lives and breathes football. It's a club with a massive heart and the managers that have got that and properly understood the size and potential of the club have been the ones who've achieved the most. Keegan understood this, Bobby understood it and Eddie absolutely gets it. But we're in a different position now than in any other period in the past.

The legendary figures that have come into the club in the past – Kevin Keegan, Bobby Robson and to some extent Rafa Benítez – have all come to us when the club has been on its knees, and have answered our prayers for salvation. But each time, their time was cut short because one of the other key components of the club wasn't working as it should.

In the Keegan era, we had a club legend, England legend and back-to-back Ballon d'Or winner in charge, an inspirational figure to the lads he managed. He saved the club from relegation, upgraded the facilities for the modern era and went about restoring pride and establishing a commitment to professionalism among his players. He brought them up to the Premier League and finished third in his first season, qualifying for the UEFA Cup. It was an incredible achievement in such a short space of time and it wasn't a flash in the pan – Keegan achieved European football for the club in 1995–96, too. He proved we could compete at the highest level. Keegan's Newcastle era was the time of 'The Entertainers', with the likes of David Ginola, Philippe Albert, Faustino Asprilla, Les Ferdinand and Alan Shearer lighting up St James' Park with free-flowing attacking football on unbelievable nights like the 5–0 thrashing of Man United in October 1996. We were the club that neutral fans wanted to watch on *Match of the Day*. We were box office. And then the club broke the world transfer record to bring Alan Shearer home. While attention was naturally drawn to big-name signings, Keegan also nurtured the home-grown talent we had coming up through the ranks, like Steve Howey, Rob Lee, Steve Watson, Robbie Elliott and Lee Clark.

In Keegan, we had a manager the players and supporters loved, a proper strategy and a focus on improving the whole training set-up. At the beginning, after some frank exchanges with the chairman, he also had the funds he needed to improve the squad. The only reason the spell was broken was because of the ruthless desire for executives to make a lot of money in a stock market flotation. I know Kevin very well. He is, when it comes down to it, one of the most decent men I've ever met. He's a man with a strong moral compass who wears his heart on his sleeve – he couldn't be a part of what the board were up to when he knew the damage it would do to other people whom he cared about.

Sir Bobby had the recipe for success at Newcastle United and brought us back to the Champions League. He was an inspiring man manager, a tireless optimist, a fighter and an unbelievably hard worker who brought the best out of those around him. As Andy Griffin said to The Athletic, 'The team was basically an extension of who Bobby was; that zest for life, that energy, that enthusiasm, that desire to win, having a sense of no fear.' He brought us incredible memories – the 8–0 thrashing of Sheffield Wednesday in his first home game, restoring Shearer from bench-warmer to game-changer, and that historic turn-around in 2002, winning three Champions League games in a row to qualify for the second group stage when we looked dead and buried. Everyone loved Sir Bobby, old and young, but towards the end of the 2003–04 season, he lost the support of a section of fans, something I neither subscribed to nor under-stood. He also had a difficult dressing room to contend with – a new generation of young men earning a lot of money and valu-ing things that were alien to a man like Sir Bobby. And on top of that, he was being left out of transfer and contract negotiations by the board. With all the key components of the club creaking, it's almost a surprise the whole thing didn't come crashing down before it did. It took what happened after Sir Bobby left for the disgruntled elements of the club to realise that they didn't know how good they'd had it.

Rafa Benítez was a high-calibre manager who got what it was to be manager of Newcastle United. He stuck with us through relegation and we roared straight back to the Premier League. Rafa didn't shy away from a fight and wasn't afraid to stick it to Mike Ashley when his promises proved to be meaningless. It felt like in the boardroom, Rafa amplified the voices of the supporters. He gave us belief. He had our backs. And so I believe he deserves his place alongside King Kev and Sir Bobby if ever Mount Rushmore was to find itself carved into the cliffs of Northumberland (or if we could stick four statues on the four towers on the Tyne Bridge).

As for Eddie Howe, a lot of fans see the similarities with Bobby Robson. They both started their managerial careers very young: Bobby was only 34 and Eddie had only just turned 30. They've also both built up reputations as exceptional man managers, finding out what makes players tick and demonstrating genuine empathy and understanding. They also began their managerial careers working with limited resources to maximise what they had in front of them. When we beat Spurs 6–1 in the 2022–23 season at home, which I'm doing my best to mention as many times as possible in the book, nine of the players that featured that day had been at the club before the 2021 takeover. Both Bobby and Eddie turned St James' Park into a fortress – under Eddie, we only lost twice at home in the league during the 2021–22 season (to Liverpool and Man City) and twice in 2022–23 (to Liverpool and Arsenal). Under Bobby, we only lost two games at home in the 2002–03 Premier League season (to

Leeds and Man United) and three in 2003–04 (to Man United, Birmingham and Blackburn). Sir Bobby and Eddie are also seen as two gentlemen of the game, partly for their charisma, charm and easy manner with the media, but also because they're fair-minded and understanding. But don't let that fool you – underneath they are both utterly determined, driven and completely obsessed with football, living and breathing it 24 hours a day. It's hard not to feel instinctively that here is a guy that Sir Bobby would have admired and got behind. I'll always remember the Twitter meme that went around in 2023 that had Bobby Robson looking down from heaven on Eddie Howe with the line: 'You'll do for me, son.'

Eddie also shares a lot with Kevin Keegan. They both special-ise in attacking, free-flowing, exciting football that gets people up off their seats. If the mid-nineties was the era of The Entertainers, then what's this one? The New Entertainers? The Transformers? But Eddie's gone above and beyond Kevin in some ways: he's built a much more solid back line. Even in our best season under Kevin – the second-placed finish in the 1995–96 season – we still conceded 37 goals, which was only the fifth-best in the league. In 1993–94, it was 41 goals against (fifth-best again) and in 1994–95 it was 47 goals conceded (sixth-best). As Kevin himself said in April 1996: 'We will be playing the same way [next season], scoring goals and letting them in, taking the plaudits and the crit-icism.' But Eddie's found a way to play the same brand of exciting football while shoring up the back line. Under Eddie in 2022–23, we conceded 33 goals all season – the equal best defensive record in the Premier League, tied with Man City. We're performing at a consistently high level everywhere on the pitch.

Eddie's more than a hybrid of the best characteristics of Kevin Keegan and Bobby Robson – he's also a pioneer, developing new ideas and creative approaches that other managers are learning from. His time away from football strengthened him in lots of ways, to pause, to reflect on his successes and failures, to consolidate, to learn. He came back stronger. It's somehow fitting that his career break was in many ways the making of him.

Eddie also has the good sense at Newcastle United to surround himself with the right people to help achieve his vision. Jason Tindall deserves an immense amount of credit for the tireless work he's put in as Eddie's right-hand man. They've been through it all together, forming a unique coaching partnership. And that togetherness is what you have to have if you're facing a battle to keep your place in the Premier League, as we were in that 2021–22 season. The second season has surpassed our wildest dreams. I'm writing this just before the start of the 2023–24 season, and I'm confident that we're not going to be looking over our shoulders, limping to the relative safety of 40 points this time. We're in the Champions League, at the top table now.

Yes, the financial clout and ambitions of the new ownership does get compared with Sheikh Mansour taking over Man City in 2008. But times have changed. Clubs can't just spend hundreds of millions on Hollywood signings and hope the players fit into the existing set-up. We're forging our own path, doing things our own way. Eddie's investing in young players, and we're going to reap the rewards of that in the long term. It feels like we're building a sustainable foundation to compete with the big boys over the next decade. It feels like a recipe for success. And it's already spreading into other areas of the club.

Newcastle United Women played their first match at St James' Park on 1 May 2022 in front of an incredible 22,134 people, who saw them batter Alnwick Town 4–0. That was a record attendance for a women's game in England, and Newcastle United Women are in the league's fourth tier! In December 2022, a crowd of 28,565 saw them beat Barnsley 2–1 in the FA Cup. That's more than Crystal Palace's (men's) average home attendance in the Premier League. Newcastle United Women had previously been a separate, independent entity (supported by the Newcastle United Foundation), but since August 2022, they're now owned by Newcastle United for the first time in their history. And it's a massively exciting time. In May 2023, they won the Women's National League Division One North. And Eddie Howe, Callum Wilson, Jacob Murphy, Alexander Isak and Kieran Trippier all sent the players heartfelt congratulation messages. Newcastle United is a dynamic, exciting place to be right now. We're on the up.

You just have to hear Eddie on the first day of pre-season training in July 2023 to get a sense of how excited he is to be back in training. You also get a sense of the expectations he's set each of his players over the summer break: 'It's good to see everybody and bring that unique feel that the lads have brought the football club, you know, the togetherness, the spirit; you can see it already and the really good attitude to the work – the lads have come back very fit because of the programmes they've been on, the various schedules that we've individualised. The test results that we got today were as good as we've seen, so really positive signs,' he told NUFC TV.

Eddie Howe is on a permanent odyssey of improving others and himself. He's learned to evolve and adapt. He is driven to succeed and any setbacks and losses he will feel more than any of us. And a difficult time of bad results will come for the club – they always do. Sometimes just half a dozen bad results can be enough to have people questioning whether you've still got it. Football managers (even really good ones) have become weirdly disposable in this era of instant gratification: a record 26 managers came and went in the 2022–23 season (and six more left in June 2023). I've got beers in my fridge that might last longer than the first Premier League managerial casualty of the 2023–24 season.

Eddie addressed the issue of dealing with a down spell, telling me: 'There will be rocky times, but if everyone understands where we're at and the journey we've been on, I think we'll be given the patience needed.' When it comes to navigating that difficult period, which we absolutely will at some point, we need to hold on to the fact that there's no one better to steer us towards a bright future.

Back in January 2008, when I was interviewing Sir Bobby Robson for the radio documentary I made in honour of his 75th birthday, Newcastle United were experiencing a really bad run, losing four games in a row, the last of which was a soul-sapping 6–0 hammering away at Man United. Here's what Bobby said to me at that time:

'We're in a club that should be top six, always, we've got a good stadium, an even better public, we sell out every match; we know our football up here. It's a place that really does need some success – it deserves it as well. We've got an amazing sporting public here and somehow somebody has to find the magic formula.'

Sir Bobby was right as always. And as I sit here writing this closing paragraph I genuinely hope that Eddie Howe is that 'somebody'. Life as a Newcastle United supporter has often been frustrating, but it's been magical as well. We're in a new place now. A happy place. Eddie deserves a huge amount of credit for the transformation that's taken place on the pitch and behind the scenes. But I think Eddie would be the first to admit that our unbelievable success so far and hopefully beyond is not just down to one person. For the first time in a generation, it's a whole club that's United.

ACKNOWLEDGEMENTS

Thanks firstly to Eddie Howe, Kevin Keegan and Alan Shearer for sparing their time to speak to me for this book. Thanks to Newcastle United for giving me a club to love and an opportunity to dream all my life. Thanks to Sky Sports for letting me do a job I've adored for the past 15 years. Thanks to everyone who's helped and supported me on my journey; the ex-players and co-commentators, the fellow journalists and broadcasters, the producers, directors, editors and indeed all my colleagues past and present. Thanks to my close toon-mad mates who told me I wasn't crazy for trying to write a book. Thanks to Oli and Nathan for helping make the dream a reality. Lastly thanks to all the fellow Newcastle United fans and football lovers who've picked this up. I hope your love affair with the beautiful game is as life-changing as mine.